**Gil G. Noam**
Editor-in-Chief

# NEW DIRECTIONS FOR YOUTH DEVELOPMENT

*Theory*
*Practice*
*Research*

fall | 2008

# Youth, Violence, and Social Disintegration

**Wilhelm Heitmeyer**
**Sandra Legge**

*issue editors*

JOSSEY-BASS™
An Imprint of
WILEY

YOUTH, VIOLENCE, AND SOCIAL DISINTEGRATION
*Wilhelm Heitmeyer, Sandra Legge* (eds.)
New Directions for Youth Development, No. 119, Fall 2008
*Gil G. Noam*, Editor-in-Chief

Microfilm copies of issues and articles are available in 16mm and 35mm, as well as microfiche in 105mm, through University Microfilms Inc., 300 North Zeeb Road, Ann Arbor, Michigan 48106-1346.

NEW DIRECTIONS FOR YOUTH DEVELOPMENT (ISSN 1533-8916, electronic ISSN 1537-5781) is part of The Jossey-Bass Psychology Series and is published quarterly by Wiley Subscription Services, Inc., A Wiley Company, at Jossey-Bass, 989 Market Street, San Francisco, California 94103-1741. POSTMASTER: Send address changes to New Directions for Youth Development, Jossey-Bass, 989 Market Street, San Francisco, California 94103-1741.

SUBSCRIPTIONS cost $85.00 for individuals and $228.00 for institutions, agencies, and libraries. Prices subject to change. Refer to the order form that appears at the back of most volumes of this journal.

EDITORIAL CORRESPONDENCE should be sent to the Editor-in-Chief, Dr. Gil G. Noam, McLean Hospital, Harvard Medical School, 115 Mill Street, Belmont, MA 02478.

Cover photograph by Sean Warren

www.josseybass.com

# Contents

# Issue Editors' Notes

THIS VOLUME examines the causes of violent behavior among young people in an international context. The analyses presented here are deliberately very different from one another and show the many forms and sources of youth violence. Each article focuses on one of the following areas: the role of public space, the institutional context (for example, police), socialization and immigration processes, the ideological context (for example, nationalism), and more generally the relevance of social disintegration for youth violence. The qualitative and quantitative studies include national perspectives and national and international comparative analyses. This volume of *New Directions for Youth Development* thus presents a comprehensive and committed approach to international social conditions and problems, including national differences and minority and majority perspectives.

The theoretical framework we refer to is social disintegration theory, which Wilhelm Heitmeyer and Reimund Anhut elucidate in the second article. This theory assembles macro-, meso-, and microlevel approaches. In contrast to other approaches, the experience of disintegration is not limited to the economic sphere but refers also to the general institutional context and the social surroundings. It is assumed that the (objective) experience or (subjective) perception of disintegration in one or more of the three dimensions of integration (social-structural, institutional, personal) causes a lack of individual recognition. The development of socially harmful attitudes and behavior is seen as one potential alternative reaction for gaining recognition. Thus, different forms of youth violence are seen as a product of social disintegration and lack of

recognition. All of the articles in this volume refer to this theoretical approach in one way or another, critically or affirmatively.

The third through fifth articles focus on the role of public space. First, Steffen Zdun compares the meaning of deviant behavior and crime in street culture in Brazil, Russia, and Germany. This qualitative study examines street culture norms and their relevance for youth groups in everyday life. Looking at youth in violent and less violent countries, Zdun highlights similarities in the reasons for violence and fear of violence coexisting with differences in frequency and intensity.

Next, Marco Oberti examines the factors explaining the wave of riots in French towns in November 2005, especially criticizing the disintegrative character of the so-called *modèle d'intègration républicaine* (republican model of integration) for people with a migrant background in French society. Using a comparative approach, he also examines the similarities and differences between the riots in November 2005 and the student movements in spring 2006. Without reducing the riots to a clash between ethnic groups with specific interests, he underlines the combination of specific sociostructural factors (such as social origin, level of education, and age) and spatial effects, which play an important role in the context of the riots by transforming inequalities in visible and unsupportable discrimination. In emphasizing the relationships of different dimensions of social inequality as sources for the riots, he develops several political and practical recommendations.

In the fifth article, we move to the topic of juvenile experience and fear of violence in three cities and two smaller towns in the north of England. Using one of the few qualitative analyses in this field, Tom Cockburn shows the main sources of fear of violence among youth. Alongside factors like young people's experiences in public spaces and the effects of alcohol consumption, Cockburn stresses the significance of the way society views youth as passive and innocent objects, whereby the juvenile perspective is consciously ignored in public policy. In this context, the author advocates a new political approach at the local level.

NEW DIRECTIONS FOR YOUTH DEVELOPMENT • DOI: 10.1002/yd

The sixth and seventh articles examine the institutional context. Taking a historical perspective, Clarissa Huguet and Ilona Szabó de Carvalho discuss institutional reasons for the criminal and violent situation in the *favelas* of Rio de Janeiro, especially the role of the police. Starting with an overview of the origins and development of violence, crime, and drug trafficking in the *favelas*, the authors show how these slums came into being. Their causal analysis focuses on the lack of integrative public power. They present the dual concept of public policy (combined with an ambivalent role of the police, which is also caused by marginalization processes), both controlling and producing violence as the crucial factor for the violent and excluded character of the *favelas*. The authors conclude by presenting the first results of a government attempt to stop the violence and improve the social opportunity structure of the residents and especially the youth of the *favelas* by means of a police unit that started operating in 2000.

The situation in the *favelas* shows that institutions cannot realize their potential as buffers between disintegrative macrotrends and the individual unless they understand themselves as an integrative machine. But where institutions produce perceptions or experiences of disintegration, the risk increases, especially among the young, that people will detach themselves from the institutional order and strive for autonomy at any cost. In the research on delinquency, need for autonomy is a core predictor for delinquency, and this relationship has been confirmed in several qualitative and quantitative studies. But the question of what makes a difference for individual variation in youths' needs for autonomy is still unanswered, or, more specifically, the reasons that some young people develop an especially strong need to be free from social control instances are largely unexplored.

Timothy Brezina addresses this research topic in the seventh article. On the basis of the multiwave Youth in Transition panel survey of male adolescents in the United States, he finds a relationship between a strong need for autonomy and delinquent behavior consistent with the findings of previous research. The empirical findings also show that lack of recognition plays a significant role for the strength of the need for autonomy. Drawing on these findings, Brezina concludes with recommendations for preventing violence.

The eighth and ninth articles focus on the influence of socialization and immigration factors on violence. Migration is often a stressful event. From the perspective of the family, the most important source of social support, it is essential to maintain social status and avoid socioeconomic decline, with consequences for the function of social support and control of children. There are also several difficulties young people have to deal with. Often they have to adapt to a new education system, make new friends, and establish a social status that guarantees sufficient recognition. In this context, migration can be considered a risk factor for crime and violence.

Gustavo S. Mesch, Hagit Turjeman, and Gideon Fishman examine the effect of migration on delinquency among young Russians in Israel. Without differentiating among specific types of delinquency—in contrast to previous work on the criminogenic effect of immigration—they investigate the effect of migration on different forms of delinquency. On the basis of the findings of survey data from face-to-face interviews with immigrant youths from the former Soviet Union in Israel, the authors reason that assimilation is not guaranteed to prevent violent acts in multicultural societies, and they develop a more sophisticated approach. The results also underscore the importance of differentiating between different types of delinquency.

Alongside the general potential effect of immigration on juvenile delinquency are the differences in the level and kind of social integration of different groups with a migrant background in a society. In Germany, Turkish and Russian immigrants are the two largest groups, and each has very different levels of integration. In contrast to Russian youths, most of the Turkish adolescents were born in Germany, but mostly without the right to German nationality, which most of the Russian youth possess. But independent of these differences, both groups show higher rates of violence than do native German youths. In the ninth article, Dirk Baier and

Christian Pfeiffer investigate the causes of the different levels of violent behavior among juvenile Russian and Turkish immigrants in comparison to German youth. Based on a large school survey, they examine the causes for the variations in the rates of violence among the different ethnic groups. The findings show that alongside the role of social integration, different cultural orientations in particular represent a core predictor of violent behavior.

The tenth and final empirical article of the volume moves on to the role of specific ideologies, such as nationalism, in explaining youth violence. In the article, Peter Sitzer and Wilhelm Heitmeyer examine the preconditions for right-wing extremist violence among German youths. As a general fact, they emphasize the significance of a mentality in society directed against socially weak groups. Without claiming a deterministic relationship, Sitzer and Heitmeyer assume that widespread negative attitudes against specific outgroups could have a legitimizing character for violent acts against these groups among right-wing extremist youths. They consider a wide range of recent quantitative and especially qualitative studies about right-wing extremist perpetrators and systematize the findings on the basis of a process model. The findings are also compatible with the basic assumptions of the social disintegration theory.

The last article of this volume discusses problems and perspectives regarding prevention and intervention programs in the context of youth violence in order to offer a potential basis for international collaborations. Kurt Möller analyzes the forms of and reasons for violence examined in the previous articles from the perspective of social work. He focuses on the implications for social praxis on the basis of the empirical findings regarding the relationship between social disintegration and violence among juveniles. After an overview of general international results, he works out some basics regarding a promising approach in the field of social work under the perspective of social disintegration theory. In this context, he stresses the significance of the establishment of a broader concept of social work to support and generate integration, life control, and competencies among young people. To guarantee not only short-term intervention but also prevention, adequate social politics and long-term perspectives are emphasized. The article concludes with a call for close collaboration of research and the praxis of social work.

## Note

We would like to thank the scientific back staff of our Institute (Martin Winands, Sylja Wandschneider, Judith Scherer, Nils Böckler, and Larissa Appelt) for their support in formatting this issue.

Wilhelm Heitmeyer
Sandra Legge
*Editors*

WILHELM HEITMEYER *is a professor of socialization at Bielefeld University, Germany, and head of the Institute for Interdisciplinary Research on Conflict and Violence.*

SANDRA LEGGE *is a researcher in the Group Focused Enmity project at the Institute for Interdisciplinary Research on Conflict and Violence at Bielefeld University.*

# Executive Summary

## Chapter One: Youth and violence: Phenomena and international data

### Sandra Legge

The topic of youth, violence, and disintegration needs addressing because young women and men are the world's greatest capital. They have the energy, talent, and creativity for building a future. But this group also suffers grave vulnerabilities. The time of adolescence includes important and difficult periods of life (for example, becoming more independent from the family, finding an adequate position in society, and starting a family of one's own). All of these points are strongly correlated with social integration, employment, and a place in the labor market—important factors in this context.

This article gives an overview of the international development and the actual situation of socially harmful behavior among youths— both fatal violence (homicide) and nonfatal violence (such as bullying, fighting, and carrying weapons). The author shows that different kinds of youth violence represent social problems in every society. The data show that youths are not only perpetrators but also the group with the highest risk of becoming victims of violence. Furthermore, the data from around the world show that their vulnerability is not limited to this sphere. It arises also from their social conditions, especially their high risk of being disintegrated from the labor market. The parallels in the data underline the significance of

NEW DIRECTIONS FOR YOUTH DEVELOPMENT, NO. 119, FALL 2008 © WILEY PERIODICALS, INC.
Published online in Wiley InterScience (www.interscience.wiley.com) • DOI: 10.1002/yd.269

a functioning institutional structure without positing a deterministic relationship between the risk of economic disintegration and violent behavior.

---

## Chapter Two: Disintegration, recognition, and violence: A theoretical perspective

**Wilhelm Heitmeyer, Reimund Anhut**

The literature explaining deviance, criminality, or violence offers a broad spectrum of approaches in criminology and sociology. Mostly the theories focus on specific levels of explanation like the macrolevel (for example, strain theories) or the microlevel (for example, self-control theory).

This article presents a relatively new theoretical approach combining different levels and focusing on three dimensions associated with specific kinds of recognition: social-structural, institutional, and socioemotional. The social-structural dimension refers to access to the functional systems of society and the accompanying recognition of position, status, and so on. The institutional dimension concentrates on the opportunity to participate in public affairs with the aim of getting moral recognition. The socioemotional dimension emphasizes the quantity and quality of integration in and social support from families, friends, partners, and so on, which provide emotional recognition.

The underlying idea is that lack of access, participation, and belonging causes a lack of recognition. When this happens, social and individual problems increase. Thus, deviant and violent behavior can be seen as one potential reaction to a lack of recognition and as a way to gain status and recognition in a different manner (for example, with a delinquent peer group or other gang).

NEW DIRECTIONS FOR YOUTH DEVELOPMENT • DOI: 10.1002/yd

## Chapter Three: Violence in street culture: Cross-cultural comparison of youth groups and criminal gangs

### Steffen Zdun

Violence is a widespread phenomenon in juvenile street culture. But the questions of whether this relationship is a deterministic one, and if not, which are the contributing factors, are largely unanswered. This article focuses on the role of public space, starting with a comparison of the meaning of deviant behavior and crime in street culture in Brazil, Russia, and Germany. Focusing on street culture norms and their relevance for youth groups in everyday life, the author shows that there are worldwide similarities, and these are most likely to be seen in disadvantaged neighborhoods. The article deals not only with the question of how people act in conflicts but also focuses on a social order in which the reputation of men is based mainly on questions of masculinity, honor, and power expressed through aggressive behavior. The results are based on more than one hundred semistructured qualitative interviews with street culture youth, prison inmates, adult family members, social workers, police, and researchers that were conducted in recent years in the three countries.

The study also describes a typology of conflict behavior among male street culture youth that helps in understanding why even juveniles who were socialized in the milieu of the street culture can reject violence and do not have to turn to violence in all conflicts. The article examines the similarities in the reasons for violence and fear of violence, as well as the differences in frequency and intensity between violent countries (such as Brazil and the Russian Federation) and less violent countries (for example, Germany).

NEW DIRECTIONS FOR YOUTH DEVELOPMENT • DOI: 10.1002/yd

## Chapter Four: The French republican model of integration: The theory of cohesion and the practice of exclusion

Marco Oberti

What are the explaining factors for the wave of riots in France in November 2005? In providing some answers, this article begins by examining the practical usefulness of the French republican model of integration for social cohesion, highlighting the way its negation of other criteria, such as ethnicity, race, or religion, limit this national conception of citizenship and emphasizing these excluded factors as one of the main causes of frustration and resentment among migrant groups in France.

The author compares these riots to the student movements in spring 2006 and shows some similarities as well as important differences between the explaining structural factors of these two youth-based social upheavals. One of the contributing distinctions is the experience of ethnic and racial discrimination as an important source of deep resentment. The author avoids reducing the riots simply to a clash between ethnic groups with specific ethnic interests or a class revolt. Instead, he stresses the relationship between specific social structural factors and spatial effects as the element that created the context for the riots by transforming inequalities into visible and indefensible discrimination. Several factors show that spatial aspects (in the form of segregation) are important alongside the ethnic/racial ones in explaining the riots.

## Chapter Five: Fears of violence among English young people: Disintegration theory and British social policy

Tom Cockburn

Young people are not only the perpetrators of violence; they are also the victims of violent acts. This leads to the question of how young people handle potential risk and how they can reduce the danger of becoming victims. The article stresses the topic of juvenile experience and fear of violence. Starting with a description of the nature of social disintegration in the north of England and the social consequences of social change at the beginning of the twenty-first century, the author focuses on the experience of young people who are affected by changes in social policies, such as the governmental response to antisocial behavior, which is generally considered to be the cause of escalating youth crime. It is pointed out that young people's experience of social disintegration is more complex than generally considered. Based on one of the few qualitative studies in this research field, the study outlines the reasons for fear of violence by presenting comments by young people in two cities and three smaller towns in the north of England. In particular, it looks at the experience of young people in public spaces, the effect of excessive alcohol consumption, young people's fears around illegal drugs and violence, strategies young people use to remain safe, and factors that tend to reduce perceived safety. The authors question the wider societal view that young people are passive and innocent objects: this view has consequences regarding the drive to reduce and avoid violence (by adult society) but also can result in increased insecurity for young people. For this reason, the article also provides a new political approach regarding the communal context.

## Chapter Six: *Violence in the Brazilian* favelas *and the role of the police*

### Clarissa Huguet, Ilona Szabó de Carvalho

Institutions should normally have an integrative influence. The family, for example, has the task of protecting and giving socio-emotional support to children, and schools should prepare young people for their future. Ideally the common goal of all of society's institutions is to secure the integration of youth and prevent or intervene against deviant behavior. But sometimes institutions provoke or even cause juvenile delinquency. The article discusses institutional influences and the role of the police in the criminal and violent situation in the *favelas* of Rio de Janeiro.

Starting with an overview of the origins and the development of violence, crime, and drug trafficking in the *favelas*, the authors show how these slums arose. Their analysis examines the lack of a state presence with an integration policy to avoid social disintegration. Instead of social integration policy, there is a dual approach that both controls and produces violence. The article also presents the first results of a government attempt in 2000 to introduce a new police unit to stop the violence and improve the social opportunity structure of the residents of the *favelas*, especially young people.

## Chapter Seven: Recognition denial, need for autonomy, and youth violence

### Timothy Brezina

Some adolescents develop an especially strong need for autonomy, desiring to be "their own boss" and determined to follow their own rules. Previous research indicates that an exaggerated need for autonomy is associated with aggression and other problem behaviors. Yet little is known about the origins of such "me-first" attitudes. Why do some young people develop a stubborn need for autonomy in the first place?

This article focuses on the role of adolescent autonomy needs in the development of youth violence, drawing on the insights of recognition theory and suggesting that the origins of an exaggerated need for autonomy can be found in the experience of recognition denial. Data from a large sample of male adolescents are used to test this hypothesis. The findings are consistent with the hypothesis, showing that perceived recognition denial (including the perception that one is treated as an inferior) contributes to a strong need for autonomy. Both are associated with elevated levels of violent behavior. The author closes with a discussion of the findings and their implications for violence prevention.

## Chapter Eight: Social identity and violence among immigrant adolescents

**Gustavo S. Mesch, Hagit Turjeman, Gideon Fishman**

Whereas traditional criminological theories treat juvenile delinquency largely as a reactive and expressive behavior that only seldom leads to specialized criminal offending or a criminal career, this article proposes an alternative classification of offenses that accounts for the difference between youthful reactive conduct and specialized criminality. It examines the effect of immigration on delinquency among juvenile Russians in Israel. In contrast to previous work that has examined the criminogenic effect of immigration without differentiating specific types of delinquency, this study investigates the immigration effect on eclectic as well as specialized delinquency. Based on survey data from face-to-face interviews with 910 immigrant youths from the former Soviet Union in Israel, the study finds important results regarding the integration of juvenile immigrants in modern societies. In contrast to the assumption that assimilation in multicultural societies represents a safe way for social adaptation and to prevent specific kinds of violent behavior, the authors find empirical support for a more sophisticated approach. Furthermore, the results underline the importance in differentiating between distinct forms of violence.

## Chapter Nine: Disintegration and violence among migrants in Germany: Turkish and Russian youths versus German youths

**Dirk Baier, Christian Pfeiffer**

Turkish and Russian immigrants are the two largest groups of immigrants in Germany, but there are some important differences regarding their legal status. Although most of the Turkish adolescents were born in Germany, few of them have German citizenship. In contrast, most of the Russian youths were born outside

Germany, but they mostly possess German nationality because of their status as ethnic Germans. Despite these differences, both groups show a high level of violent behavior. This article investigates the causes for the different levels of violent behavior among juvenile Russian and Turkish immigrants in comparison to German youths. On the basis of a large-scale school survey with 14,301 respondents, the authors examine the causes for their high level of violent behavior compared to German adolescents. The theoretical basis is a combination of disintegration and socialization theory, as well as additional factors that are discussed as causes of violence in several theoretical approaches.

In the empirical part of the article, the authors provide a systematic description of sources and levels of disintegration among the three youth groups. The empirical findings demonstrate that juvenile migrants are more disintegrated in several respects and that the higher level of disintegration explains some of the differences in violent behavior. But specific cultural orientations are also important in this context.

## Chapter Ten: Right-wing extremist violence among adolescents in Germany

Peter Sitzer, Wilhelm Heitmeyer

What are the preconditions for right-wing extremist violence among German youths? For several years, the rate of this violence has been increasing in Germany, and the same can be observed for right-wing extremist orientations characterized by the coming together of ideologies of unequal worth and the acceptance of violence as a mode of action. And although it is emphasized that approval of and willingness to use violence do not automatically lead to actual acts of violence, this article suggests that the existence of these convictions in society helps to legitimize attitudes that become expressed in violence, in particular among youths.

This article presents a five-stage process model that portrays the underlying preconditions for acts of right-wing extremist violence, the contexts in which such violence takes place, and the factors that cause it to escalate. This structural model is used to outline central empirical findings of recent German quantitative and especially qualitative studies about right-wing extremist violent offenders. For analytical reasons, the basic elements of the process model (socialization, organization, legitimation, interaction, and escalation) are treated separately. The authors also examine right-wing extremist violence from a disintegrative perspective. Given that intersubjective recognition is an existential human need, right-wing extremist violence is understood as a "productive" way of dealing with individual recognition deficits. On the basis of the integration dimensions of social disintegration theory, three fundamental recognition needs are distinguished. Right-wing extremist violence can best be explained as a consequence of recognition deficits in all three central integration dimensions.

## Chapter Eleven: The role of social work in the context of social disintegration and violence

### Kurt Möller

Violence and the violence discourse are very similar from country to country: focus on youth, preponderance of males among perpetrators and victims, disproportionate involvement of migrants and indigenous people, greater prevalence with socioeconomic disadvantage and low education, and the impact of underlying factors such as political disintegration, exclusion from the consumer lifestyle, and inadequacies of social institutions. In social disintegration theory, the basic explanatory backdrop is the dynamic relationship of integration and disintegration between and within the different spheres: individual and functional system integration, integration into society, and integration into the community. (Relative) exclusion from work, consumption, and democratic processes combined with experience of socioemotional deficits seem to give a particularly strong boost to socially unacceptable forms of particularist integration and to favor collective and individual acceptance of violence. When subjects draw balances of personal recognition and of the achieved and achievable scope to organize their life, the latter orientations appear subjectively more likely to meet their expectations than socially (more) accepted modes of behavior.

The central conclusion on social reactions to violence in general and professional social work in particular is that rather than relying on admonishment, punishment, or curative measures, or some combination of these, to combat violence, there is a need for wide-ranging long-term options for those acutely affected and at risk to have the long-term scope to organize their own lives—to experience life control, recognized integration, and development of competences. Those who experience being the organizer of their own life have no need of violence as a form of self-assertion.

*Although young people are society's capital, a global perspective indicates their vulnerability not only regarding the practice and experience of violence but also in relation to their social integration in general.*

# 1

# Youth and violence: Phenomena and international data

*Sandra Legge*

VIOLENCE IS A WIDESPREAD PHENOMENON around the world. According to the *World Report on Violence and Health*, there is no country or society without this social problem. In 2000, about 1.6 million people lost their lives through violence—a rate of 28.8 per 100,000. More than half of these cases were suicides, one-third were homicides, and one-fifth were caused by armed conflicts.[1] Thus, about 520,000 people, or 8.8 per 100,000, were killed by interpersonal violence.[2] Males represented 75 percent of all homicide victims. On a world scale, the highest homicide rate—nearly 19.4 per 100,000—was found among males between the ages of fifteen and twenty-nine. The rate tends to decrease with age among males while remaining stable among females (at 4 per 100,000).[3] Alongside individual factors such as sex and age, rates of violent death also depend on country income levels, being more than twice as high in countries with low to middle income (for example, 32.1 per 100,000 in Africa and South America) as in countries with high income (14.4 per 100,000).[4]

NEW DIRECTIONS FOR YOUTH DEVELOPMENT, NO. 119, FALL 2008 © WILEY PERIODICALS, INC.
Published online in Wiley InterScience (www.interscience.wiley.com) • DOI: 10.1002/yd.270

There are global similarities as well as great regional differences in youth homicide rates. One general finding is that these rates among youth aged ten to twenty-four increased in many parts of the world between 1985 and 1994. Homicide rates increased among males in general, and especially among youth aged fifteen to nineteen and aged twenty to twenty-four. In 2000 about 199,000 youths—or 9.2 per 100,000—were victims of fatal violence. With the prominent exception of the United States, with a juvenile homicide rate of 10 per 100,000, most of the affected nations are developing countries, characterized by economic and social conflicts, weak social security systems, great income inequality, and a culture of violence.[5] Africa and Latin America have the highest homicide rates of youths, whereas Western Europe, parts of Asia, and the Pacific region show the lowest.[6] Furthermore, studies show that for every youth homicide, there are between twenty and forty victims of nonfatal violence whose injuries need hospital treatment. And in some countries, for example, Israel, New Zealand, and Nicaragua, the ratio is even higher. Nonfatal violence includes bullying, carrying weapons, and physical fighting, all of which may lead to more serious forms of violence.[7] As with fatal youth violence, the majority of perpetrators of nonfatal violence are males.

Physical fighting, bullying, and carrying of weapons are very common among school-age children in many countries. For example, studies show that about one-third of school students have been involved in fights, with the rates for boys two to three times higher than for girls. The same difference can also be observed for carrying weapons, where the ratio is still greater. For instance, in Cape Town, South Africa, 9.8 percent of males and 1.3 percent of females in secondary schools reported having taken a knife to school during the preceding four weeks. A national survey of pupils in grades 9 to 12 in the United States found that 17.3 percent had carried a weapon in the previous month, and 6.9 percent had carried one in school.[8]

Taken together, these examples show that youth violence is a serious and widespread problem around the world. And although there are significant differences in the rates of violence between countries and regions, there is also a common strand: youth are not only the main perpetrators of such violence but also the main victims, with high costs for the society in question. So it is all the more important to find explanations that can lead to ways to reverse this trend.

The scientific literature provides a wealth of approaches, which focus on different levels of explanation: individual, situational, social, cultural, and economic factors.[9] However, none of these risk factors can explain the entire phenomenon on their own (one need only consider the findings of the studies reported in this volume). But one factor stands out: the importance of the socioeconomic status of the family and of youth in general.[10] As White puts it, "The social ecology of poverty, and prevalence of youth employment in particular, is crucial for understanding the precise nature and extent of juvenile offending in particular locales. Youth unemployment is the foundation for . . . criminality. . . . More generally, the extent of inequality in access to community resources, especially income opportunities, is essential to youthful offending."[11] Thus, especially for youth, access to the labor market is a crucial factor because in many cases, work opens further opportunities to realize personal needs such as starting a family, autonomy, recognition, and participation in society. But a look at the global situation concerning the economic integration of young people reveals evidence of the increasing economic vulnerability of children and youth. A child born in the twenty-first century has a four in ten risk of living in extreme poverty.[12] In both developed and developing countries, young people are especially affected by poverty.[13]

The highest child poverty rates are in the developing countries.[14] Among industrialized countries, the Russian Federation, where every fourth child is poor, has the highest rate of child poverty, although rates in Western countries are also high. For example, almost 17 percent of young people in the United States live in poverty, and the figures are similar in Canada, Australia, and Italy; the figures in France, Germany, the Netherlands, and the United Kingdom are just under 10 percent. Only Belgium and Scandinavia have child poverty rates under 5 percent. There are also differences in poverty rate trends. Whereas child poverty rates have fallen in Canada, Norway, the United States, and the United Kingdom since the late 1980s and remained unchanged in the Netherlands,

Belgium, and Sweden, there were clear increases in Hungary, Mexico, Italy, West Germany, and Finland.[15] Chen and Corak show that the observed changes in child poverty rates are caused not only by family and demographic forces but especially by changes in the labor market and government support.[16] At the same time, these results demonstrate that the increasing insecurity caused by globalization does not affect all countries, regions, organizations, and individuals equally. Country-specific factors, institutional settings, and the social structure represent important determinants of how people are affected by increasing uncertainties. In this context, the institutional structure can be considered an intervening variable between macrolevel global forces and microlevel individual responses, with the success or failure of economic integration having a great impact on the individual's life course.[17]

Young people especially are confronted with increasing difficulties when they enter the labor force. Between 1995 and 2005, the labor force participation rate decreased globally from 58.9 to 54.7 percent. Consequently, in 2005, only every second young person globally was participating in the labor market. The youth unemployment rate was 13.5 percent, compared with 4.5 percent for adults.[18] The highest regional youth unemployment rate is in the Middle East and North Africa, at almost 26 percent, followed by non–European Union (EU) Central and Eastern Europe and Commonwealth of Independent States countries (nearly 20 percent). The lowest rates (around 13 percent) can be observed in the developed economies, including the EU, which are at the same time the only regions with a marked decrease. Nonetheless, youth in these countries were still more than twice as likely to be unemployed than adults. In Southeast Asia and the Pacific, the risk of unemployment was more than five times higher for youth than for adults.

Furthermore the International Labour Office estimates that more than 20 percent of the employed youth are young working poor, which means living in a household with less than a dollar a day per head (in 2005), while approximately 47.3 percent live at the level of two dollars a day. Working poverty among youth is especially prevalent in sub-Saharan Africa and South Asia, while youth working at the level of two dollars a day decreased most in regions of Central and Eastern Europe (non-EU) and in East Asia.[19] And although young people do not represent a homogeneous group, some results can be classified as general risk factors. First, in almost all countries, economic integration is even more difficult for young women than for young men, and the unemployment rate among ethnic minorities is also higher in most countries. This is due not only to a lower level of education among these groups but also institutional discrimination. Furthermore, the unemployment rate tends to decrease with age and is likely to be higher among youth whose family has a low socioeconomic status. Regarding the level of education, the findings are somewhat different. Whereas employment and the probability of obtaining a full-time job are higher among better-educated young people in member countries of the Organization for Economic Cooperation and Development, this correlation is not necessarily a given in developing countries. Especially in parts of the Middle East and North Africa, unemployment tends to be higher among youths with better education because of the lack of jobs in the service sector.[20] In any case, "There is a proven link between youth unemployment and social exclusion."[21]

The data show that young people are especially affected by economic disintegration. They are not only perpetrators of violence but also its main victims.

On the basis of these data, one might find some parallels between economic disintegration and the experience and practice of violence among young people. But no one should leap to the conclusion that there is a simple causal relationship between these two social problems; the phenomenon is larger. Several factors can lead to juvenile violence, sometimes on their own but mostly in interaction with others. Despite these complex combinations of circumstances, we should note that the institutional structure plays an important role for social integration of youths and protection against violent acts as a buffering effect—especially between an inability to find employment and the sense of vulnerability, uselessness, and idleness among young people.[22] The institutions that might have the most influence on the life courses of youths are the family, the educational system, the social welfare system, and the employment market. Thus, several studies found that nations with stronger social welfare policies have lower homicide rates,[23] whereas in nations without a functional differentiated welfare system, economic and social inequality were closely linked with homicide rates.[24] In contrast, functional institutional systems guarantee social support and social capital.[25] And although they do not prevent violence, these factors reduce the probability that violence will occur.[26] Policies that challenge youth and people in general without providing any security are neither fruitful nor desirable for the prevention of and intervention against crime, while policies to protect and support youths during that specific period of life are both.

## Notes

1. World Health Organization. (2002). *World report on violence and health*. Geneva: Author.

2. At the same time it must be remembered that official homicide statistics do not fully capture all violent acts. World Health Organization. (2002).

3. Apart from the age group five to fourteen, where the rate is lower (2 per 100,000). In contrast, suicide rates tend to increase with age for both sexes. The highest rate, with 44.9 per 100,000, was found among men aged sixty or older.

4. In contrast, the highest suicide rates are in Europe and the western Pacific region, where they are, respectively, nearly three and six times higher than the homicide rates. World Health Organization. (2002).

5. World Health Organization. (2002).

6. Homicide rate per 100,000 population among youth (ten to twenty-nine years) in countries explicitly considered in this volume: Brazil (1995), 32.5; France (1998), 0.6; Germany (1999), 0.8; Israel (rate not calculated); Russian Federation (1998), 18.0; United Kingdom (1999), 0.9; United States (1998), 11.0. The date in parentheses indicates the most recent year that data are available. World Health Organization. (2002).

7. For some of the countries considered in this volume data are available on the frequency of bullying behavior among students aged thirteen years in 1997 and 1998: France: 49.1 percent (sometimes), 6.6 percent (weekly); Germany: 60.8 percent (sometimes), 7.9 percent (weekly); Israel: 36.4 percent (sometimes), 6.6 percent (weekly); United States: 34.9 percent (sometimes), 7.6 percent (weekly).

8. World Health Organization. (2002).

9. See, for example, World Health Organization. (2002); White, R. (2002). Youth crime, community, development, and social justice. In M. Tienda &

W. J. Wilson (Eds.), *Youth in cities: A cross-national perspective* (pp. 138–164). Cambridge: Cambridge University Press.

10. World Health Organization. (2002).

11. White. (2002). p. 146; See also Polk, K., & White, R. (1999). Economic adversity and criminal behavior: Rethinking youth unemployment and crime. *Australian and New Zealand Journal of Criminology, 32*(3), 284–302.

12. UNICEF. (2000). *Poverty reduction begins with children.* New York: Author. In this context, child poverty means more than a low family income. It also includes the experience of developmental deprivation, which may have lifelong impacts. See UNICEF. (2005). *The state of the world's children: Excluded and invisible.* New York: Author. http://www.reliefweb.int/rw/lib.nsf/db900SID/EVOD-6K3EBT?OpenDocument.

13. UNICEF. (2001). *The state of the world's children.* New York: Author. Although poverty in industrialized countries does not have the same meaning as in developing countries, where many people have to live on one dollar or less a day and where many children die before their fifth birthday. See UNICEF. (2005).

14. Belsey, T., & R. Burgess. (2003). Halving global poverty. *Journal of Economic Perspectives, 17*, 3–22. UNICEF. (2004). *The state of the world's children, 2004.* New York: Author.

15. National Center for Children in Poverty. (2000). Child poverty rates have improved since 1993, but one in six U.S. children is poor. *National Center for Children in Poverty News and Issues, 10*(3), 1; *Süddeutsche Zeitung* (German newspaper). (2007). In Deutschland leben 2,5 Millionen Kinder in Armut. No. 264, 63, 1; Chen, W.-H., & Corak, M. (2005). *Child poverty and changes in child poverty in rich countries since 1990.* Innocenti Working Paper 2005–02. Florence: UNICEF, Innocenti Research Centre. http://www.unicef-irc.org/publications/pdf/iwp_2005_02_final.pdf; Tienda, M., & Wilson, W. J. (2002). Comparative perspectives of urban youth: Challenges for normative development. In M. Tienda & W. J. Wilson (Eds.), *Youth in cities: A cross-national perspective.* Cambridge: Cambridge University Press.

16. UNICEF. (2005); Chen and Corak. (2005).

17. Mills, M., & Blossfeld, H.-P. (2005). Globalization, uncertainty and the early life course: A theoretical framework. In H.-P. Blossfeld, E. Klijzing, M. Mills, & K. Kurz (Eds.), *Globalization, uncertainty and youth in society.* London: Routledge.

18. The youth unemployment rate is the percentage of youth who are actively looking for work but not able to find any. See International Labour Office. (2006). *Global employment trends for youth.* Geneva: Author.

19. International Labour Office. (2006).

20. International Labour Office. (2006).

21. Mills & Blossfeld. (2005); International Labour Office. (2005).

22. International Labour Office. (2006).

23. Esping-Anderson, G. (1990). *The three worlds of welfare capitalism.* Princeton, NJ: Princeton University Press; Messner, S. F., & Rosenfeld, R. (1997). Political restraint of the market and levels of criminal homicide: A

cross-national application of institutional-anomie theory. *Social Forces, 75,* 1393–1416; Savolainen, J. (2000). Inequality, welfare state, and homicide: Further support for the institutional anomie theory. *Criminology, 38,* 1021–1042.
   24. Mills & Blossfeld. (2005).
   25. Cullen, F. T., & Wright, J. P. (1997). Liberating the anomie-strain paradigm: Implications from social-support theory. In N. Passas & R. Agnew (Eds.), *The future of anomie theory* (pp. 187–206). Boston: Northeastern University Press; Hagan, J., & McCarthy, B. (1997). Anomie, social capital, and street criminology. In N. Passas & R. Agnew (Eds.), *The future of anomie theory* (pp. 124–141). Boston: Northeastern University Press.
   26. Hagan and McCarthy. (1997).

SANDRA LEGGE *is a researcher in the Group Focused Enmity project at the Institute for Interdisciplinary Research on Conflict and Violence at Bielefeld University.*

*Being socially integrated means more than having a good job. Social disintegration theory unites objective social-structural, institutional, and socioemotional dimensions with subjective forms of integration and recognition.*

# 2

# Disintegration, recognition, and violence: A theoretical perspective

*Wilhelm Heitmeyer, Reimund Anhut*

THE BIELEFELD DISINTEGRATION approach, explored in this article, centers on explaining diverse phenomena of violence, right-wing extremism, ethnocultural conflicts, and devaluation and repulsion of weak groups. From a conflict theory perspective, each can be viewed as a specific, problematic pattern of dealing with states of individual or social disintegration. Disintegration marks the failure of social institutions and communities to deliver basic material needs, social recognition, and personal integrity. The disintegration approach accordingly explains these phenomena as resulting from a society's unsatisfactory integration performance.

One basic assumption of the disintegration approach is that the probability and intensity of violent behavior increase in line with experiences and fears of disintegration, while the ability to control them decreases. No direct, determinist connection at the individual level is assumed; instead, individual factors, milieu-specific

Parts of this article were published in Anhut, R., & Heitmeyer, W. (2006). *Disintegration, recognition and violence.* http://www.cahierspsypol.fr/RevueNo9/Rubrique2/R2SR1. htm

mobilizations, and opportunity structures determine the choice of specific patterns of coping (apathy and resignation also being conceivable "solutions"). Social disintegration theory (SDT) highlights different kinds of integration and disintegration and expands the idea of goal-means discrepancy into noneconomic areas where lack of recognition plays an important role.

---

## Social recognition: The basis of SDT

From the disintegration perspective, recognition comes about as a consequence of solving the problem of social integration. Following and developing initial thoughts by Bernhard Peters,[1] the disintegration approach takes the social or societal integration of individuals and groups to mean a successful relationship between freedom and attachment in which three specific problems are solved satisfactorily (see Table 2.1). This means we are dealing with three dimensions.

The social-structural dimension (individual-functional system integration) refers to participation in society's material and cultural goods. This kind of integration into the system is guaranteed by sufficient access to work, housing, education, and consumer goods. Its necessary subjective counterpart is the individual's satisfaction with his or her occupational and social position. In this context, it is not only the material situation that is important. The social aspect is also relevant, as are individual satisfaction with one's own activities and the experience of positional recognition regarding one's own position, roles, and field of activities.

The institutional dimension (communicate-interactive social integration) refers to institutional and political (forms of) participation. A balance has to be struck between conflicting interests without wounding people's integrity. From the disintegration perspective, this calls for adherence to basic democratic principles that guarantee the (political) opponent's equal moral status and are accepted as fair and just by those involved. However, the negotiation and formulation of these principles in individual cases also pre-

**Table 2.1. Integration dimensions, integration goals, and criteria for assessing successful social integration**

| Integration dimension | Individual-functional system integration | Communicative-interactive social integration | Cultural-expressive social integration |
|---|---|---|---|
| Operationalized as a solution to the following tasks | Participation in the material and cultural goods of society | Balancing conflicting interests without harming the integrity of others | Establishing emotional relations between persons for the purpose of making sense, self-realization, and ensuring socioemotional support |
| Assessment criteria | Access to employment, housing, consumer goods, and so on (objective subdimension) | Opportunities to participate in political discourse and decision-making processes (objective subdimension) | Recognition of personal identity by the group and the social environment |
| | Esteem for occupational and social position (subjective subdimension) | Willingness to participate (subjective subdimension) | Recognition and acceptance of group identities and their respective symbolism by other groups |
| | | Adherence to basic norms that ensure a balance of interests and moral recognition (fairness, justice, solidarity) | |
| Forms of recognition | Positional recognition | Moral recognition | Emotional recognition |

*Source:* Anhut, R., & Heitmeyer, W. (2000). Desintegration, Konflikt und Ethnisierung. Eine Problemanalyse und theoretische Rahmenkonzeption. In W. Heitmeyer & R. Anhut (Eds.), *Bedrohte Stadtgesellschaft. Gesellschaftliche Desintegrationsprozesse und ethnisch-kulturelle Konfliktkonstellationen.* Weinheim: Juventa. P. 48.

suppose corresponding opportunities and willingness to participate on the part of those involved. Problems of disintegration arise when individuals perceive a loss of moral recognition because of feelings of powerlessness and insufficient realization of basic norms.

Finally, the socioemotional dimension (cultural-expressive social integration) concerns collective and private aspects of life. Here we are dealing with establishing emotional and expressive relations between people for the purpose of self-realization and making sense of life. This calls for considerable degrees of attention and attentiveness, but also for space to be oneself and balancing of emotional support with normative demands so as to avoid crises of meaning, disorientation, lowered self-esteem, loss of values, identity crises, and loss of emotional recognition.

These three forms of integration are required: social-structural integration (for example, having a job), institutional integration (for example, voter participation), and socioemotional integration (for example, social support by family, friends). Clearly the disintegration approach discusses the establishing of social integration as a voluntary matter. In modern society, this characteristically takes place by balancing interests, recognition, and consensus building rather than by the earlier forms of integration in traditional societies, where a subjective sense of belonging frequently tended to be based on nonvoluntary mechanisms such as duress and pressure to conform. The disintegration perspective sees the successful accomplishment of these tasks as resulting in positional, moral, and emotional recognition and self-definition as belonging to the relevant social group. On the basis of social integration, voluntary acceptance of norms can also be expected. In contrast, in states of disintegration, the effects of one's own action on others no longer have to be taken into account. This encourages the development of antisocial attitudes and creates a risk that violence thresholds will be lowered.

## Social processes and the effect of disintegration

Which social processes does the disintegration approach consider to be responsible for an increase or decrease in social integration or a loss of recognition, and which effects are associated with the experience of social disintegration or a loss of recognition?

An increase or decrease in the degree of social integration and the accompanying changes in recognition options only provisionally expresses the extent to which the potential for dysfunctional ways of coping with disintegration is expanded or reduced. The forms of coping that individuals choose are determined by the coincidence of their experiences (competencies, patterns of accountability, and so on) with specific opportunity structures such as integration into social milieus (group pressure, compulsion to conform) and the function of the chosen pattern of behavior in compensating for lack of recognition.

In order to answer the question as to the functionality of the chosen pattern of behavior in compensating for lack of recognition, we must be clear how losses of recognition work. Three basic active principles can be identified: (1) avoidance of inferiority and harm to self-esteem, (2) restoration of norms, and (3) lack of alternative learning processes.

In the social-structural dimension, social polarizations reduce access opportunities and achievable gratifications in individual-functional system integration. An additional process of individualization propagates the concept of individuals as autonomous, competent, and successful, thereby intensifying the pressure on people to present themselves as successful. Yet despite the pressure to acquire status, the opportunities and risks of social positioning are spread unevenly. This leads increasingly frequently to disappointment for the losers in the modernization process; it unleashes feelings of resignation, impotence, and rage and causes a lack of positional recognition that undermines self-confidence. That is why people tend to endeavor to avoid this kind of harm.

There are several possibilities for coping with this situation. It has been known since the early 1930s from studies of unemployment research that apathy and resignation are the dominant patterns of reaction to experiences of this kind.[2] Another option for maintaining a positive self-image in the face of ongoing stress is to blame others for one's own fate (the scapegoat phenomenon) and to invoke prejudice and hate in order to compensate. Finally, violence is a possible outlet to compensate for feelings of weakness or to maintain a sense of self-esteem. There is thus a wide range of possible functional solutions to lack of recognition.

Institutionally, ideas of rivalry and competition at school and work, instrumental work and social relationships, and a consumer-oriented lifestyle driven by wealth, status, and prestige encourage self-interested tendencies like having to get one's own way, social climbing, and exclusion. This situation is aggravated by the change in political climate that has been evident since the 1980s, which appears to favor the teaching of egocentric, competition-oriented attitudes and to promote patterns of behavior that destroy solidarity.[3] Here we find two dominant forms of lack of moral recognition. First is the feeling that one's own life is not of equal value and that one is denied equal rights, such as nonmembership in social groups or nonacceptance in the case of formal membership of groups or society. Second is the impression that basic principles of justice are being violated—for instance, where the individual feels that he or she or his or her own group makes a relevant contribution to the collective social good yet still experiences treatment as an inferior. In addition to cases where the individual feels he or she has been treated disadvantageously or unjustly, we must also include cases where the person is not disadvantaged but formulates the feeling of injustice on behalf of others. Here, violence may be employed as an option for restoring justice (the restoration of norms—for example, Tedeschi and Felson's "restore justice" principle in 1994), or to regain respect (assertion of identity).[4] Unlike the "avoid inferiority/damage to self-esteem" pattern of motives, however, this is not necessarily done at the cost of persons or groups susceptible to discrimination; rather, it tends to be aimed against persons or groups who appear to be privileged. The expressive violence of young migrants in the suburbs of French cities whose actions say "look, we exist, we are not rats" is an example of the latter phenomenon (see the article by Oberti in this volume).

On the socioemotional dimension, ambivalent individualization processes lead to growing instability in relationships between couples, as a result of which family disintegration can have a harmful effect on the conditions in which children are socialized. The emotional stress on parents is caused especially by the combination of individuals increasingly demanding relationships based on equal rights while simultaneously experiencing many forms of inequality. This emotional stress often leads to frustration, insecurity, and a generally higher potential for tension and conflict. Unstable family relationships in turn detract from children's self-experience and the recognition that is required to build a positive self-image.[5] Consequently, aggressive and autoaggressive tendencies and conspicuous behavior in children can be directly connected to the extent of family disintegration. Denial of emotional recognition means experiencing no or too little esteem or attention in important intimate social relationships, receiving no emotional support in situations of emotional stress, to having no contact person to discuss problems with, to have no autonomy (see the article by Brezina in this volume), and so on.

In relation to the question of how affinity for violence originates, particularly in children and juveniles (and how it is subsequently reproduced in adulthood), two paths appear to be significant. First, direct learning of violence can be observed, including in the form of a repeatedly reinforced cycle of violence in which experiences of violence in childhood and the subsequent use of violence against family members in adulthood are repeated.[6] Alongside this form of direct learning from role models is a second form, which can be labeled as the lack of alternative learning processes. Violence is employed as a pattern of dealing with conflict because other means of coping are unavailable due to the lack of specific social competencies and the existence of development deficits such as lack of empathy, identity disorders, and disorders of self-esteem. In this case children do not learn a constructive model for integrating negative feelings and for being able to deal with them in a constructive way. Development deficits in the shaping of relationships, systematic overtaxing, low tolerance of frustration, a low sense of self-esteem, and vulnerability are the consequence.

Children in these situations are relatively helpless in the face of difficult family and school relationships and may turn to violence to defend themselves, compensate for weakness, or retain even meager self-esteem.[7] However, to consider this only from the aspect of learning theory would not go far enough. Even if learning is based directly on experience and models, the reproduction of behavior is not necessarily attributable solely to the learning process. At the same time, it has been shown that those who break out of the cycle of violence (the nonrepeaters) had at least one person during childhood in whom they could confide their worries or went on to live in a fulfilling partnership.[8] Here, too, it is evidently the existence of emotional recognition that determines the version or reproduction of the pattern of behavior, which is why basic learning theory is in urgent need of expansion to include a recognition theory perspective.

It is thus possible to identify three basic principles of the effect of violation of recognition: the quest to avoid injuries to self-esteem, the need to restore norms and assert identity, and the lack of an alternative pattern for dealing with conflict. However, as yet, no preliminary decision has been taken as to which pattern of reaction will emerge in an individual case. As we have seen, violence can become a pattern of coping with problems regardless of the specific causes of lack of recognition.

This raises the fundamental question as to the nature of specific configurations of effects, for example, whether specific lack of recognition in certain integration dimensions predisposes some people to specific patterns of reaction. In principle, three configurations of effects are conceivable.

First, it could be that lack of recognition that stems primarily from one integration dimension also causes one specific pattern of reaction. For instance, while rivalry and subjective feelings of disadvantage might be primarily responsible for xenophobia, national-authoritarian or right-wing extremist attitudes are chosen because they are the best means of combating disorientation and feelings of impotence, and individual readiness to resort to violence essentially springs from the experience of severe corporal punishment, psychological humiliation, and a hostile social environment. This would mean that the choice of a particular pattern of coping depends primarily on which pattern of coping promises to most effectively limit or compensate for the recognition deficit that has arisen.

Second, it would be imaginable that in principle, every pattern of coping could be a reaction to different prior losses of recognition. In that case, a possible nucleus of loss of recognition would emerge only

NEW DIRECTIONS FOR YOUTH DEVELOPMENT • DOI: 10.1002/yd

in the choice of specific variations of a pattern of reaction. With regard to the disintegration approach, Albrecht, for instance, considers it conceivable that recognition deficits in the social-structural dimension are primarily responsible for the risk of status-securing violence (for example, procuring status symbols), that disregard experienced in the institutional dimension is a key factor in politically motivated and collective violence (for example, xenophobic violence), and that all kinds of emotional deprivation give rise to identity- and esteem-securing violence (tests of courage, and so on).[9]

Plausible as this proposal sounds in terms of a macroperspective or reconstruction of the causes of violence, it still raises the question as to whether this pattern of thinking does not also involve parceling out recognition, in which case earlier questions regarding similar classifications would resurface. One could imagine distinguishing among instrumental violence (harming the victim is only a means to an end based on a nonaggressive need), emotional violence (aimed at reducing internal states of tension based on an actual need for aggression), and expressive violence (the primary form of violence in the case of self-presentation). One criticism of these classifications is that it is often impossible to draw a clear distinction, since the different causal patterns (in the case of emotional-reactive aggression primarily hostile and violent treatment by the environment, in the case of instrumental aggression the existence of successful models or the person's own successes with aggressive behavior) may coincide in each individual case.[10]

Hence, there is much support for the third pattern of interpretation, according to which it seems to be possible to compensate for lack of recognition in individual integration dimensions by recognition gains in other dimensions. In that case, the crucial factor would be the balance of recognition. The choice of a specific pattern of action or a variation of it would then no longer be attributable to a specific lack of recognition in one or more integration dimensions. That would mean that although the chosen pattern of coping was subjectively the one that the person expected to have the biggest effect in a given situation, the person's experiences, competencies, and patterns of accountability, along with individual and social opportunity structures, such as integration into social milieus, were likely to be of crucial significance in deciding which choice was ultimately made.

---

## Reactions to denial of recognition

Several researchers have pointed out that it is important to identify which criteria are relevant for explaining when individuals react with deviant behavior and when they do not. How should one imagine or conceptualize the correspondence between recognition or integration theory on the one hand and specific kinds of deviant behavior on the other? In an attempt to find a provisional answer to this question, we suggest that three groups of moderating variables are significant for this relationship: social competencies, patterns of accountability, and social comparison processes (see Anhut and Heitmeyer 2006).

In relation to social competencies, a simple logic seems identifiable from a deficit-theory perspective. This is that the better that individuals are equipped with social competencies, the less susceptible they seem to be to dysfunctional patterns of coping. Consider the pattern of indirect learning of violence in which violence was classified as a symptom of lacking social competence (lack of empathy, identity disorder, lack of self-esteem). However, the findings here are not always as unambiguous as researchers would like them to be, since groups of persons with high self-esteem and an apparently stable sense of self-esteem have often been found to have an affinity with violence.[11] Baumeister and Bushman also doubt whether there is a causal relationship between a low sense of self-esteem and aggression as a pattern of action, since they see a person's unwillingness to allow feelings of shame as the key to aggression, and this tends to apply more to people with high self-esteem than to those with low self-esteem. Accordingly, they say that violent patterns of action are most likely when people with a positive self-image come across people who attack their assessment of themselves and that the most susceptible are people with a high but unstable sense of self-esteem.[12] However, aggressive people who react emotionally are subjectively more keenly aware of threat than nonaggressive people are, which raises the question whether it is possible to construe a subjective sense of threat and aggression independent of each other.

With patterns of accountability, at first sight clear patterns of classification suggest themselves. Causes of disruption or obstruction of objectives can be localized elsewhere. Individual attribution of responsibility, whereby people attribute the cause of failure to themselves, would tend to suggest depoliticizing patterns of coping (apathy, withdrawal). Social policy attributions of responsibility would tend to encourage disenchantment with politics and rejection of the system, for example, or even new, solidarity-based patterns of behavior. Collective patterns of accountability place the responsibility for a social problem with one or more social groups, which favors collective forms of reaction (prejudices, discrimination, scapegoating). Although the principle of the effect of the patterns of accountability appears very clear, problems arise from the fact that the type of accountability can also fulfill a function for the receipt of recognition. With respect to the type of action we use as an example, violence, Schmidtchen has pointed out that in situations where the individual can no longer tolerate a specific degree of self-contempt, self-contempt turns to contempt for the social environment so that he or she is able to bear the pressure on his or her own personality.[13] Therefore, especially in extreme situations when the recognition issue touches on existence, one may no longer be able to assume accountability principles functioning in normal circumstances.

As for the role of social comparison processes, we must assume that these processes not only relativize a person's own state of integration (and hence the balance of recognition) but that in many cases, they should not be construed as independent of the question of integration at all. Every judgment of a state of integration ("Am I integrated?" "Am I treated with respect?" and so on) that is not a self-addressed temporal comparison ("Am I treated differently now than I was before?") is already the outcome of a social comparison process. Therefore, social comparison processes must be included conceptually in the operationalization of integration or disintegration.

---

## Conclusion

Investigating the role of social integration or disintegration for the use of violence requires considering more than just the fact of employment integration. Integration comprises economic, institutional, and socioemotional dimensions that are capable of producing sufficient individual recognition in different societal spheres. The studies presented in the following articles are discussed from this theoretical perspective.

### Notes

1. Peters, B. (1993). *Die Integration moderner Gesellschaften*. Frankfurt am Main: Suhrkamp.
2. Eisenberg, G. (2002). Die Innenseite der Globalisierung: Über die Ursachen von Wut und Hass. *Aus Politik und Zeitgeschichte, 44,* 21–28.
3. Hengsbach, F. (1997). Der Gesellschaftsvertrag der Nachkriegszeit ist aufgekündigt: Sozio-ökonomische Verteilungskonflikte als Ursache ethnischer Konflikte. In W. Heitmeyer (Ed.), *Was hält die Gesellschaft zusammen? Bundesrepublik Deutschland: Auf dem Weg von der Konsens- zur Konfliktgesellschaft* (Vol. 2, pp. 207–232). Frankfurt am Main: Suhrkamp.
4. Tedeschi, J. T., & Felson, R. B. (1994). *Violence, aggression and coercive actions*. Washington, DC: American Psychological Association.
5. Peuckert, R. (1997). Die Destabilisierung der Familie. In W. Heitmeyer (Ed.), *Was treibt die Gesellschaft auseinander?* (pp. 287–327). Frankfurt am Main: Suhrkamp.
6. Schneider, U., Lösel, F., & Selg, H. (1990). Erstgutachten der Unterkommission Psychologie. In H.-D. Schwind (Ed.), *Ursachen, Prävention und Kontrolle von Gewalt* (Vol. 2). Berlin: Dunker & Humboldt.
7. See, among others, Ratzke, K., Sanders, M., Diepold, B., Krannich, S., & Cierpka, M. (1997). Über Aggression und Gewalt bei Kindern in unterschiedlichen Kontexten. *Praxis der Kinderpsychologie und Kinderpsychiatrie, 3,* 152–168.
8. Ratzke, K., & Cierpka, M. (1999). Der familiäre Kontext von Kindern, die aggressive Verhaltensweisen zeigen. In M. Cierpka (Ed.), *Kinder mit aggressiven Verhalten: ein Praxismanual für Schulen, Kindergärten und Beratungsstellen* (pp. 25–60). Göttingen: Hogrefe.

9. Albrecht, G. (2003). Sociological approaches to individual violence and their empirical evaluation. In W. Heitmeyer & J. Hagan (Eds.), *International handbook of violence research* (pp. 611–656). Dordrecht: Kluwer, 639.

10. Compare Nolting, H. P. (2002). Lernfall Aggression: wie sie entsteht– wie sie zu vermindern ist; ein Überblick mit Praxisschwerpunkt Alltag und Erziehung. Reinbek: Rowohlt.

11. For example, Helsper, W. (1995). Zur, Normalität jugendlicher Gewalt: Sozialisationstheoretische Reflexion zum Verhältnis von Anerkennung und Gewalt. In W. Helsper & H. Wenzel (Eds.), *Pädagogik und Gewalt: Möglichkeiten und Grenzen pädagogischen Handelns* (pp. 113–154). Opladen: Leske & Budrich.

12. Baumeister, R., & Bushman, B. (2003). Emotions and aggressiveness. In W. Heitmeyer & J. Hagan (Eds.), *International handbook of violence research* (pp. 479–493). Dordrecht: Kluwer.

13. Schmidtchen, G. (1997). Wie weit ist der Weg nach Deutschland? Sozialpsychologie der Jugend in der postsozialistischen Welt. Opladen: Leske & Budrich.

WILHELM HEITMEYER *is a professor of socialization at Bielefeld University, Germany, and head of the Institute for Interdisciplinary Research on Conflict and Violence.*

REIMUND ANHUT *is a senior researcher at the Institute for Interdisciplinary Research on Conflict and Violence at Bielefeld University, Germany.*

*Although there are many similar values and norms of street culture in Brazil, Germany, and the Russian Federation, there are also quite a few differences concerning the use of violence and crime by street culture youth.*

# 3

# Violence in street culture: Cross-cultural comparison of youth groups and criminal gangs

*Steffen Zdun*

THIS ARTICLE COMPARES ATTITUDES TOWARD violence and crime in juvenile cliques and criminal gangs in street culture in Brazil, Germany, and the Russian Federation. The patterns of the street code are similar worldwide and are observed especially in disadvantaged neighborhoods. In this milieu, people are socialized by rules of social interaction that differ from middle-class norms. There are, however, differences among these countries concerning the intensity and frequency of violence. To explain the differences and similarities, I combine my own results with insights from a comparative review of recent literature on Brazil, Germany, and the Russian Federation.[1] I discuss my findings from the perspective of the Bielefeld disintegration approach of Anhut and Heitmeyer.[2]

My arguments are based on about one hundred semistructured qualitative interviews of juvenile offenders and experts from the three countries and a content analysis of at least one hundred studies. I

present some of the main findings. It is beyond the scope of this article to present quotes from the interviews, explain my methodology, and refer to all studies of my comparative review.[3]

---

## Street culture norms in youth groups

I use the term *street culture* in the sense defined in Anderson's seminal work on disadvantaged neighborhoods.[4] Anderson explains that people in this milieu have their own set of values and norms. Those who want to be treated with respect cannot show weaknesses in everyday life and run away from problems. Every challenge demands an (aggressive) reaction to defend one's reputation. A person who cannot or does not want to respond in this way (and especially if this person calls the police) is socially isolated. Thus, an important peculiarity of street culture is the way that people deal with conflicts.

Men and women of street culture milieus grow up with these norms and learn to reject insults and servile attitudes—even if they deal with them in different ways. For men, it is crucial to establish an image of masculinity by defending their honor and the honor of others, especially their mother. They try to impress others by showing off their physical strength or seek to achieve reputation and power in other ways.[5] It is not enough for them to be seen as tough; they must constantly demonstrate their toughness.[6] Their peers are the relevant source of masculine recognition.

Youth who have few other life possibilities compete for reputation and self-esteem; they use physical aggression against others or provoke them into starting a fight. This is also stressed by the disintegration approach, which argues that violence is "a possible outlet to compensate for feelings of weakness and/or to maintain one's sense of self-esteem."[7] Alternative ways of social positioning are status symbols, drug use, and weapons.

From the male point of view—and in many countries, from the female too—men are the defenders and women should not use violence. In some countries, such as the United States, women try to gain respect by behaving in similar ways to the men.[8] They want to challenge traditional gender stereotypes. This behavior is not just about gaining a reputation; it is also about creating an image of strength that provides security because aggressive women have less trouble than shy ones do.[9]

However, in many other countries, women are allowed to turn to violence only when they are alone and have to defend themselves. Nevertheless, even in such cases, men demand the right of revenge afterward. Connell hence argues that male street culture behavior is meant to keep women away from the "serious games" of gaining social power.[10] In other words, the relationship between the genders is based on domination and power. The right to fight becomes a question of power—the power to deal with conflicts and to control one's girlfriend.

It is important to note that these attitudes could not persist if women did not accept them. Women may dislike being repressed and seeing how their partner gets beaten up or wounded and may ask him not to fight, but many women in this milieu accept the violence of their partners for protection when they feel threatened. Especially in countries where everyday life is aggressive, such as Brazil and the Russian Federation, it is easy to see why this is necessary. The level of violence against women is much higher than in Western Europe, and many street culture women have been the victims of rape or attempted rape. They want a male defender. Mothers also accept that their children internalize the street code for self-defense. So it is not only the influence of peers and fathers wanting their friends or sons to become "real men" that keeps street culture active across the generations.[11]

Even in street culture, violence is not the only way to resolve conflicts, and recognition is based on more than fighting. Youth of street culture milieus are a heterogeneous group and deal with conflicts in various ways. Nevertheless, certain regional aspects define the range of variation. In the disadvantaged areas of big cities in Brazil and Russia, for instance, juveniles often need not only close friends with whom they share a strong sense of solidarity, but also strong friends who are able to protect each other against rivals. So even young men who largely reject violence can become associated with aggressive youths in their neighborhood for protection.[12] This protection is necessary not just against aggressors from outside but also against people from their own neighborhood. For example, a youth who rejects the demands of gang members may face serious consequences. This kind of solidarity is about costs and benefits and cannot be compared with the emotional bond of friendship. Thus, the solidarity of youth groups in such neighborhoods is often overestimated, for instance, in terms of collectivism.[13]

In less violent countries such as Germany, where the protection of a strong clique is less important, the situation is different. Strong friends are seldom necessary, and whether one gets involved in serious conflicts is more a matter of choice. Normally only provocative individuals who create conflicts on their own regularly get into such situations. For the others, it happens only by accident.[14] Another important issue in dealing with conflicts is the choice of victims and enemies. Both of them are predictable under attack. Perpetrators are often able to treat victims as they want because the latter are too afraid to defend themselves and call for help. Attacks on victims are mainly about getting money or favors, or simply for the pleasure of the tormentor. In contrast, conflicts with enemies who play the game at the same level as the aggressor are about gaining recognition. So enemies and victims play different roles in street culture conflicts. In addition, there are also "rejecters": those who know the street code but avoid conflict and will call the police. They are normally seen as neither victims nor enemies and do not become part of the "game" because they are less attractive for the aggressors. For the same reason, people from the middle class are rarely involved in street culture conflicts. Their calm and deescalating behavior is seen not just as a weakness, but also as proof that they are ill suited for this kind of conflict.

The distinction among enemies, victims, and outsiders can be explained by the functional character of conflicts. First, the function of conflict relates to the benefits that fights with well-chosen enemies and victims provide. Even though fights could be avoided, for instance, when one side is willing "to back down, apologize, and/or make sufficient amends," this will not happen when both parties are concerned about their reputation.[15] Second, well-chosen enemies and victims will not inform the police after a fight. This, of course, helps to avoid arrests.

This explanation can be combined with Richard Felson's concept of routine activities.[16] According to his theory, people who are interested in engaging in conflict deliberately put themselves in situations and go to places where they expect their need for conflict to be satisfied. Since these are usually likely to be locations where they meet other people who are also interested in conflict, it is not surprising that many conflicts take place between like-minded members of street cultures.

In addition, as Miller explains, these conflicts have to be interpreted from the point of view of the street culture youth.[17] Their deviant behavior is often an interaction with an end in itself rather than a revolt against the middle class and its norms. In other words, if middle-class people get attacked, they were generally in the wrong place at the wrong time or reacted in the wrong way.

I found geographical differences concerning the choice of adversary. In the Russian Federation, where every encounter with the police can bring problems, even for victims, there are many reasons to avoid any kind of encounter with security forces. People can be beaten, mistreated, or forced to give money to corrupt police. In contrast, in German street culture, juveniles do not have to be so afraid of the police. Furthermore, the justice system works differently there. Young offenders have to be involved in several offenses before they can be detained. Moreover, first-time young offenders usually are required to do community service or they receive a suspended sentence. These kinds of punishment may work for some young people and give first offenders a better chance for the future. Aggressive street culture youth, however, are not usually impressed by such penalties. Some provocative individuals sometimes attack outsiders because they are not afraid of punishment.[18]

The Brazilian laws for children and youth have similar effects. The criminal records of children and juveniles are erased from their files after their eighteenth birthday. Moreover, their penalties are sometimes just socioeducational measures in "educational centers," and the sentence has to be less than three years. Educational centers are comparable with prisons but are not called prisons because it is not an official form of prison. The main intention is to withdraw the youth from circulation. This system of punishment turned out to be crucial for Brazilian crime rates because a lot of street culture crime is committed by children and youth.[19]

An oddity of these laws is that a person who commits a crime shortly before turning age eighteen will not be punished at all: after turning eighteen years old, they cannot be judged under juvenile law—but they cannot be tried under adult law for a crime committed as a juvenile either. We can assume that rather than preventing crime, such laws may encourage juveniles to attack rivals.

The code and operation of street culture should not be misunderstood as fairness. The idea of fairness here is a myth. Opponents are chosen by specific criteria, but it is not important to fight against a well-matched adversary. A group will attack a single member of a rival group, for example. So it is important for a group member to avoid passing through rival territory alone.[20]

Such unequal fights are not even regarded as illegitimate. They are just seen as the fault of the outnumbered group or member and as part of their long-term conflict in which one act of revenge is followed by another. And as the brutality of the battles increases, the original cause of the conflict normally gets forgotten.

In many countries, street culture youth rivalries can be observed between different ethnic groups. However, this ethnic violence in many cases reflects a functional selection of adversaries rather than conflicts based on interethnic warfare. First, the juveniles normally fight against youth of their own origin as often as against other ethnic groups. Second, they usually concentrate their attacks on the street culture youth of specific ethnic groups. For instance, Russian German migrants prefer Turkish youth for conflicts in Germany. The number of conflicts with autochthonous Germans is significantly smaller—even though the migrants feel socially excluded and discriminated by the autochthonous population—because many autochthonous Germans would call the police after a fight.[21]

## Criminal gangs

Especially in Brazil and the Russia Federation, there are connections between youth groups and criminal gangs within the milieu of street culture. Here we focus on the peculiarities and similarities of criminal gangs in the three societies.

One major similarity is the relevance of territories. These are not just a place to live but also the area where gang members conduct their business. Thus, rivals seeking to take over a group's territory represent a large danger. Brutal conflicts can even lead to the death of the inferior party. In Brazil and Russia, that means that the more important the illegal business gets, the more intense and violent the conflicts on territories become.[22] Hence, disadvantaged neighborhoods controlled by drug factions are often in a state of permanent conflict with each other. Takeovers occur to enlarge a territory or prevent further attacks by rivals. In addition, changes in the leadership of a territory because of betrayal and drug wars are part of everyday life. Drug wars affect not just the members of the gang and the residents of their territories but the entire population of the city because innocent people can be caught in crossfire when they pass these neighborhoods.

Nevertheless, gangs typically try not to affect life beyond the borders of their territory too much. Their main interest is their illegal business. As long as this business is running properly, they earn good money, so theft and robbery are not attractive for them. Theft and robbery bring in small amounts of money in comparison to the narcotics business, trading in weapons, and prostitution, and the risk of being caught by the police is much higher. For this reason, muggers and robbers are often poor people or junkies who want to buy drugs. Although the drug factions profit from their robberies indirectly, they try to avoid this kind of crime and too much violence close to their territories. Otherwise they face the risk that the police will enter the neighborhoods to stop these offenses, and this would not just reduce the number of robberies but also endanger their drug trade.

To that extent, the gangs are interested in harmony—inside and outside their territory—because every conflict is bad for their business. The drug factions often even act like an informal police force within their territories. If a resident is robbed or attacked by someone else, the gangs will punish the offender. In addition, gangs sometimes give money to poor people, especially to buy medicine. Local residents do not have to pay for this assistance, but they do have to help the drug dealers against the police, for example, by hiding them during a raid.[23]

The positive image of gangs and the growing instability of family relationships in countries such as Brazil and the Russian Federation also influence the recruitment of new members. Children in disadvantaged neighborhoods see gang members every day and notice how rich and powerful they are in contrast to their own parents. The gang members become a substitute for the family and are seen as role models because they have found a way to get respect. The children and juveniles of these neighborhoods are aware that they will never get this kind of respect unless they join the drug factions.[24] According to disintegration theory, this has "a harmful effect on the conditions in which children are socialized."[25] Due to a lack of guidance by the family, they lack "the recognition that is required to build a positive self-image" that fosters the copying of attitudes and behavior within the peer group.[26] Although gang members often face a shortened life, many children see getting involved with them as attractive. They start by providing small services for a gang, and in the process try to get noticed and gain a position within the hierarchy. They hope to live long enough to become the leader or at least to gain respect and all the benefits of established gang members.[27]

This means that both intrinsic and extrinsic reasons play a role in the decision to join a criminal gang. Poverty, poor living conditions, family problems, and the need for protection against arbitrary, corrupt, and brutal police forces in these neighborhoods are one part of the explanation. To understand the other reasons behind such a choice, we also have to consider social recognition, social control, the dynamics of group processes, and individual attitudes. If only the extrinsic reasons mattered, everyone who lived in these neighborhoods would have to be involved or at least be interested in being involved. But this does not happen in Brazil, the Russian Federation, or Germany. Children and juveniles in Germany simply face fewer risk factors and are less likely to join criminal gangs than juveniles who live in more violent environments.[28]

Because recognition is one reason to join gangs, it is worthwhile to have a look at hierarchies. Three types predominate: military command structures, corporate structures, and horizontal structures.[29] Their design differs according to regional and cultural factors, but these differences refer only to the division of tasks within a gang and say nothing about the brutality of a gang or the type of violence it prefers to engage in.

In Brazil, military command structures with hierarchical systems are most common. Each *favela* has one *dono*, who is in charge of controlling the managers of a *favela* and the *soldados* in his territory. The latter protect the *favela* against other drug factions and the police. They are also responsible for taking over other *favelas*. The managers of a *favela* control the managers of the *bocas* (the places where drugs are sold in the *favela*). The managers of the *bocas* in turn control the drug dealers who sell the drugs in the area around a *boca*. Last but not least, there are children and women who wait at strategic points, like at the entrances to a *favela*, to signal to the others if the police or other gangs are about to enter.

Such strict military command structures are rare in the Russian Federation. Organized armed gangs do operate in various neighborhoods, but there is normally just one leader who has some advisers he can trust. The advisers are responsible for making sure that the commands of the leader are fulfilled. Further specialization and hierarchy are not common.[30] Criminal gangs in Germany have a similar structure to those in Russia, with the major differences being that the German gangs have almost no influence on politicians and that the economy of the country depends less on illegal markets. In contrast, in Russia, as in many other violent countries such as Brazil, there are strong ties between illegal business and politicians, the police, the justice system, and the economy. Not every person is involved in this, but all layers of the society seem to be affected by illegal business because of corruption.

Another relevant issue is the age at which young people join a gang. In the Brazilian *favelas*, it is normal for children aged about ten to join; at the age of twelve, they carry weapons. The problem is that they often have not yet developed the ability to control their actions by this age; moreover, many of these children have been victims of violence within their families. According to the disintegration approach, this fosters violence as well as "problems in recognizing one's own feelings and the feelings of others and in reacting empathetically to them."[31] Besides this, children who are nervous, or aware of peer pressure, or on drugs can be careless around guns. As a result, the level of brutality and homicide rates have skyrocketed in countries with younger armed gang members. This can be observed in Russia as well as in Brazil, although the number of armed children in criminal gangs in Russia is neither as large as nor growing as quickly as in Brazil.[32] Whereas the Brazilian *favelas* are now often controlled by juveniles and young adults, adults still control illegal business in Russia and normally use minors only as helpers. In Germany, membership in criminal gangs is irrelevant for most children and juveniles in disadvantaged neighborhoods.[33]

In general, German criminal gangs do not get much help from the residents in their neighborhoods. And because they are not needed for protection and social services, they hide their identity and their business. And although they make a lot of money by selling drugs and engaging in other illegal activities, being attached to a gang does not seem to be attractive to many young people. Typically there are no ties between aggressive youth cliques and the criminal gangs in German disadvantaged neighborhoods.

Because of this division in Germany, we should take a closer look at the differences between aggressive youth groups and criminal gangs. In Brazil and Russia, the gangs are attractive because they offer protection, recognition, and career options that young people who join them could not achieve on their own. In contrast, German criminal gangs offer no protection against dangers of everyday life, and indeed they bring the risk of gaining a bad reputation. Moreover, membership is a risky career option alongside others.

In addition, the interests of aggressive youth groups and criminal gangs vary. Many aggressive juvenile gangs use violence to gain social recognition and for their own amusement. In contrast, criminal gangs use just as much violence as necessary to control the business because they do not want to be disturbed by the police. In other words, the members of criminal gangs in Germany are professionals who care primarily about their income. They view social recognition as more about power and money than about violence. Therefore, German criminal gangs have little to offer to the street culture juveniles, who are attached to an aggressive clique to get respect and attention.[34]

## Competition and illegal business

Another important issue is the competition for resources in disadvantaged neighborhoods. Residents are excluded to a large extent from the social life of "middle-class-society." This situation increases the likelihood that they will join criminal gangs and earn money in the black economy and also the likelihood that they will lose faith in the idea of equality in society.

Another dimension of competition relates to the fact that the illegal business is not regulated by law. It is based on trust and the threat of violence. The problem is that in any given city, there will be a limit to the demand for any particular illegal product. This level of demand does not change much, and there is competition among criminal gangs. One way to solve this problem would be for the gangs to decide that everyone will get a share. But human nature always leads each to want as much as possible, so the gang members fight each other to gain more profit.[35]

Furthermore, in Brazil and the Russian Federation, there is not just competition among the criminals but also a corrupt police force that participates in the illegal business: police officers are bribed to not disturb the business, and some police are dealers as well. Some of them sell illegal goods—not only drugs—and weapons to the criminals, and others run their own businesses. For instance, after the fall of the iron curtain, many former generals and members of the secret service in the former eastern bloc states began running illegal businesses and used their former infrastructures to become rich and powerful.[36]

The trade in illegal products is just one part of their business today. Another is security: they are blackmailers who take protection money. The situation that juvenile victims face is just one dimension of this phenomenon. Young blackmailers ask their victims to pay not to be tormented. Criminal gangs act in the same way, only they earn much more money by blackmailing shops and restaurants. One peculiarity of the Russian Federation concerning this business is that "protection services" became so widespread in the 1990s that today they are often legal and even pay taxes. Companies that had to be forced to pay money before now accept them as an alternative to dealing with crime in a weak and corrupt country where violent offenses are a part of everyday life.[37] Here, the criminal gangs are in competition with state institutions.

The biggest problem is that private security services guarantee security only for companies and privileged individuals, and the state monopoly on violence is lost. In turn, the sense of security and trust in the police and the justice system is also lost.[38] The result of this process is a demand for more private security. People of the upper and middle classes are able to afford this and do everything to get protection. Especially in violent countries such as Brazil and the Russian Federation, they build private housing complexes surrounded by walls, electric fences, and armed guards.[39]

People of the lower classes of these countries, however, face a great deal of danger and have little help from the authorities. They cannot afford private security and so depend on local gangs. But because the gangs are in competition with other gangs and state institutions, they rarely provide much in the way of protection. In fact, they often cause insecurity. Isolated from the mainstream institutions, people who live in gang territories usually are responsible for their own security.[40] This is another dimension of inequality that weakens the social cohesion of a society, a concept from Anhut and Heitmeyer's disintegration approach.

The situation is different in Germany, where the gap between social classes is less extreme than in Brazil and the Russian Federation. In Germany, the social welfare system reduces the sense of inequality within society. Furthermore, the state monopoly on violence is still widely accepted, and state institutions are trusted because they work much better than they do in violent countries. Nevertheless, even in Germany, the demand for private security forces and security systems is increasing, an indication of a decreasing sense of security that may weaken the state monopoly on violence. In addition, other processes of social disintegration are visible, such as problematic social interactions concerning intimate relationships, the socioemotional bond within families, and the socialization of children.

## Conclusion

Violence in street culture has many causes and channels of legitimization, and some of its aspects can be explained by the Bielefeld disintegration approach. The approach especially helps us to understand the meaning of social recognition for the use of violence.

Juvenile group violence in street culture differs from criminal gang violence in violent countries such as Brazil and the Russian Federation and less violent countries such as Germany. Across the world, the norms and values of street culture and the reasons conflicts start are similar, but the frequency and intensity of violence differ. One reason for the differences is that everyday life in violent countries is so harsh that even people who are not interested in fights can regularly get involved in them. In less violent countries, it is much easier to avoid them. Another difference between violent and less violent countries is that in the latter, there are only weak ties joining criminal gangs, politicians, state institutions, and the economy. This differs from the relatively strong ties in violent countries, which is what enables illegal business to function without much state interference. In turn, the state monopoly on violence and the sense of security is lost. Private security services become responsible for the security of companies and privileged people, and criminal gangs control the disadvantaged neighborhoods and their security. Such developments are observed only at a low level in low-level violent countries.

In addition, we have to consider the relevance of socioeconomic integration within a society. This refers not just to poverty and unemployment but also to competition between the social classes. In violent countries, people from the upper and middle classes are often afraid of those from the lower classes. They avoid them and tend to stigmatize their milieu as criminal. This is because those who live in disadvantaged neighborhoods in such countries often depend on criminal gangs and help them against the police at times. Nevertheless, it would be wrong to conclude that most lower-class people are criminal. Nevertheless, the upper and middle classes ignore both this fact and their own responsibility for the situation. Indeed, they exploit the situation to justify continuing to keep the lower classes away from the social and financial resources. The result is increasing social and economic polarization between the classes, as well as increasing competition within street culture.

This culture of exclusion, stigmatization, locking away, and ignoring the problems of others is based on fears that stand in a reciprocal relationship with economic and social problems. Economic problems foster feelings of insecurity that lead to more social problems, which have a negative influence on the economy and lead to more fear.[41] General improvements in different areas of a society are needed to prevent such downward spirals. In contrast, single interventions often have only temporary effects on the symptoms of a problem and provide no long-term changes in the root causes.

If those in power simply assign blame and do not react actively, such downward spirals may occur even in countries that still have a relatively low level of violence today, such as Germany. I have shown that the structures and rules of street culture are similar worldwide. When phenomena of crime such as found in Brazil and the Russian Federation also become virulent in less violent countries, the key factors seem to be the social and economic situation, the existence of a functioning social welfare system, and the authority of the state.

## Notes

1. In Germany, my research was based on a migrant group, Russian Germans; more than 2.4 million people have immigrated since the late 1980s. Because of their number, lack of language skills, and own norms, they have difficulty integrating into German society. They are one of the most interesting groups for research on street culture in Germany because the code of the streets is common to this group. My interviews with them provided information about street culture in Germany and the Russian Federation and identified differences between the countries.

2. Anhut, R., & Heitmeyer, W. (2006). *Disintegration, recognition and violence.* http://a.dorna.free.fr/RevueNo9/Rubrique2/R2SR1.htm

3. For more details about the results and the methodology, see Zdun (2007). *Ablauf, Funktion und Prävention von Gewalt: Eine soziologische Analyse gewalttätiger Verhaltensweisen in Cliquen junger Russlanddeutscher.* Frankfurt; Zdun, S. (Forthcoming). *Indicators for culture of violence*: Peter Lang Verlag.

4. Anderson, E. (1990). *StreetWise: Race, class, and change in an urban community.* Chicago: University of Chicago Press.

5. MacYoung, M. (1992). *Violence, blunders, and fractured jaws.* Boulder, CO: Paladin Press.

6. Stewart, E. A., Schreck, C. J., & Simons, R. L. (2006). "I ain't gonna let no one disrespect me": Does the code of the street reduce or increase violent victimization among African American adolescents? *Journal of Research in Crime and Delinquency, 43,* 427–458.

7. Anhut & Heitmeyer. (2006).

8. Hagedorn, J., & Devitt, M. (1999). Fighting females: The social construction of the female gang. In M. Chesney-Lind & J. Hagedorn (Eds.), *Female gangs in America.* Chicago: Lakeview Press.

9. Jones, N. (2004). "It's not where you live, it's how you live": How young women negotiate conflict and violence in the inner city. *Annals of the American Academy of Political and Social Science, 595,* 49–62.

10. Connell, R. W. (1995). *Masculinities.* Cambridge: Polity Press.

11. Zdun. (2008).

12. Zdun. (2008).

13. Agnew, R. (2006). Storylines as a neglected cause of crime. *Journal of Research in Crime and Delinquency, 43*(2), 119–147.

14. Zdun. (2007).

15. Agnew. (2006). p. 129.

16. Felson, R. (1987). Routine activities and crime prevention in the developing metropolis. *Criminology, 25,* 911–931.

17. Miller, W. B. (1958). Lower class culture as a generating milieu of gang delinquency. *Journal of Social Issues, 24*, 5–19.

18. Zdun. (2007).

19. Dowdney, L. (2002). *Child combatants in organized armed violence.* Rio de Janeiro: 7 letras.

20. Zaluar, A. (2001). Violence in Rio de Janeiro: Styles of leisure, drug use, and trafficking. *International Social Science Journal, 53*, 369–378.

21. Zduni. (2007).

22. Dowdney. (2002); Shlapentokh, V. (1999). A multi-layered society in contemporary Russia: Criminals and oligarchs as its major actors. *Research in the Sociology of Work, 8*, 93–115; Volkow, V. (2000). Gewaltunternehmer im postkommunistischen Russland. *Leviathan, 28*, 173–191; Zaluar. (2001).

23. Dowdney. (2002).

24. Zaluar. (2001).

25. Anhut & Heitmeyer. (2006).

26. Anhut & Heitmeyer. (2006).

27. Dowdney, L. (2005). *Neither war nor peace. International comparison of children and youth in organised armed violence.* Rio de Janeiro: 7 letras.

28. Zdun. (2008).

29. Dowdney. (2005).

30. Shlapentokh. (1999).

31. Anhut & Heitmeyer (2006).

32. Soares, L. E., Bill, M. V., & Athayde, C. (2006). *Cabeça de Porco.* Rio de Janeiro: Editoria Objectiva; Zdun. (2007).

33. Kinzig, J. (2004). *Die rechtliche Bewältigung von Erscheinungsformen organisierter Kriminalität.* Berlin: Duncker & Humboldt.

34. Zdun. (2008).

35. Dowdney. (2002).

36. Dunn, S. (1994). Major mafia gangs in Russia. In P. Williams (Ed.), *Russian organized crime: The new threat?* (pp. 63–87). London: Frank Cass.

37. Shlapentokh. (1999). Both the Russian Federation and Brazil face a vacuum of institutional security. After decades of communism in Russia and dictatorship in Brazil (1964–1985), they are young democracies. The strong hand of the state that took control of most spheres of public life in the past has difficulty controlling violence and crime today.

38. Anderson (1990) argues, concerning disadvantaged American neighborhoods, that a lack of faith in the criminal justice system is one of the main reasons that people lose trust in the state and its institutions.

39. Davis, M. (2006). *Planet of slums.* London: Verso.

40. Stewart et al. (2006).

41. Although some industries such as the security business and gun manufacturers profit from this.

STEFFEN ZDUN *is a research associate at the Institute for Interdisciplinary Research on Conflict and Violence at Bielefeld University, Germany.*

*Urban segregation is a crucial topic in explaining recent riots in France. It brings together the ethno-racial and social dimensions, reinforcing the feeling of discrimination.*

# 4

# The French republican model of integration: The theory of cohesion and the practice of exclusion

*Marco Oberti*

FOR THREE WEEKS between the end of October and mid-November 2005, a wave of riots shook more than two hundred towns in France. Beginning in the eastern suburbs of Paris following the deaths of two adolescents who believed they were being pursued by the police, the riots spread across the country. Less than six months later, a large youth movement mobilized against a new measure introduced by the Dominique de Villepin government in response to the November riots—the "First Job Contract" (*Contrat Premier Embauche*, CPE).[1] Strikes and blockades of universities began in February while the law was still under discussion in parliament. Three-quarters of French universities were blockaded or had classes interrupted as a result of the movement. In March 2006, these blockades spread to secondary schools, over a thousand of which were affected by collective action.

This article was translated from the French by Brian Shevenaugh of DePaul University, Chicago.

NEW DIRECTIONS FOR YOUTH DEVELOPMENT, NO. 119, FALL 2008 © WILEY PERIODICALS, INC.
Published online in Wiley InterScience (www.interscience.wiley.com) • DOI: 10.1002/yd.273

Simultaneously, an intense round of demonstrations began across the country.

This article focuses more on the riots than on the student movement, using the comparison between these two social movements to reflect on the social cohesion in a society that boasts a strong integration model. In fact, the so-called *modèle d'intégration républicaine* (republican model of integration) was barely mentioned in terms of its capacity to maintain social cohesion after the riots.[2] Essentially, this model is based on a national conception of citizenship that negates using certain criteria (such as ethnicity, race, or religion) to categorize individuals and to treat them as specific groups. In theory, this means that the state interacts with the individual independent of these criteria, which implies equal treatment for all. This is the reason the state refuses to recognize interest groups and official public institutions that are based on these criteria. In addition, there is a restrictive conception of *"laïcité"* (secularism) that prohibits religious practices and identities from appearing in the public sphere and restricts them to the private sphere. I will also reflect on the methodological and theoretical aspects of analyzing this kind of social movement, as well as its impact on public policies designed to foster integration in France.

This comparison is relevant because both movements were based on mass youth mobilizations. Nevertheless, youth in both groups differed not only in their academic, social, ethnic, and urban characteristics, but also in terms of the individual and collective action they turned to: violent confrontations with the police and repeated destruction and vandalism of public and private goods in one case; strikes, street protests, university sit-ins, and political mobilization in the other. This comparison is a way of examining the recourse to violence as a mode of expression and of making individual and collective demands.

The context of segregation and social vulnerability in which the riots took place can be seen as the root of disintegration. However, issues of social recognition also can be used to explain the violence that occurred.[3] In this way, recourse to violent forms of expression by working-class urban youth (often of immigrant background) should be linked to the strength of the resentment they feel when they are faced with the contradictions and dead-ends of the republican model of integration.[4]

## Characteristics of the French republican model

This model[5] is based on a national concept of citizenship that negates using certain criteria (such as ethnicity, race, or religion) to categorize individuals and treat them as specific groups.[6] In theory, this means that the state interacts with the individual independent of these characteristics, which implies equal treatment for all. This is the reason the state refuses to recognize interest groups and official public institutions based on these criteria. In addition, there is the restrictive conception of *laïcité* (secularism).

School, health, and housing are classic public services that must disregard these differences. For example, school is viewed as a basic institution with a social integration function that is supposed to guarantee equal opportunity independent of social, ethnic, and religious background. The idea is that being French means accepting being a part of this national community of citizens and relegating the dimensions of individual identity to the private sphere. This is the reason that alternative forms of this social model are rejected. It also explains why social and ethnic segregation is perceived as a danger to social cohesion.

This position implies that everyone in France has equal opportunities no matter where they live. For a long time, the state claimed to guarantee relative homogeneity of the conditions required to maintain social integration and equality of opportunity for all, although this was not actually the case.

Historical and economic conditions made this model of republican integration relatively efficient. Despite war and conflict related to decolonization, the period following World War II (1945–1975) was a sort of golden age for this model: economic growth, expansion of the welfare state, belief in progress, strong political and trade union representation of the working class, and high upward social mobility all favored strong social integration.[7] Although conflict and violence accompanied the integration of early- and mid-twentieth-century European immigrants, the next generation—the baby boomers whose children were born in France—took advantage of this period. Not only were they able to become French citizens, but they were also integrated at school and work. Thus, theirs was an experience of social mobility. If segregation, stigmatization, and discrimination had plagued their parents, they themselves were less affected.

I do not want to overemphasize the contrast between the *trente glorieuses* and the most recent period of the crisis that began in the 1970s. This model has always been an ideal and was never completely realized. Nevertheless, economic growth, the belief in a better future, and a strong working-class movement gave it consistency and credibility. Labor shortages created by the reconstruction and modernization of France led to the arrival of the first immigrant generations from the former colonies, in particular from North Africa. This first wave of immigrants, mainly composed of men, arrived in France with an intent of returning home eventually. They were crammed into slums and bore the full weight of rejection by French society, which was bogged down in the Algerian war and other conflicts linked with decolonization. These immigrants faced difficult social conditions, such as finding work and adequate housing.[8] Moreover, their position as "foreigners" from former colonies meant they were regarded as second-class citizens. This generation's experience with humiliation and exploitation is part of a collective memory that is still prevalent in the third generation.

During the 1970s and 1980s, the possibility of returning to their country of origin diminished. As these immigrants settled permanently, the *regroupement familial* (reunification of the family in France as a justification for residence there) came into being. Thus, the second generation of migrants was born and socialized in France. Unlike early-twentieth-century European immigrants, these second-generation North Africans have been penalized not only by a sluggish economy but also because of their ethnoracial characteristics. The gap between what the French republican model implies—meritocracy, rights, and citizenship—and their actual situation is one of the major causes of the frustration and resentment that young French people feel. Theirs has been an experience of stigmatization, segregation, and discrimination (racism) based on their African backgrounds and the social fragility that they and their parents share. In some cases, Islam or violence has become a way for them to express their discontent and reclaim their ill-treated dignity and identity.[9]

This immigrant background is a crucial aspect of the French context, but we cannot reduce the riots to this single cause.

## The autumn 2005 riots and the spring 2006 student movement

In their interpretations of these urban riots in 2005 and 2006, most foreign media focused on the issue of multiculturalism and the role of Islam in France. Some journalists went so far as to compare these events to those that took place in Los Angeles in 1992, thus promoting an overly racialized interpretation of the riots.[10] Others were quick to stigmatize Muslims as being "hostile to the rules and customs of Western countries." The difficulty French society has had with integrating Muslim immigrant populations—or even its inability to do so—was thus highlighted. By extension, the challenge that multiculturalism poses for France would appear to come down to religion: that of the difficulty Islam would have in finding its place in a society characterized by Christianity and a secular political culture. Better-informed foreign commentators viewed these events as a revolt of the most deprived groups, composed of people who are immersed in deep social despair and faced with a waning French republican model that has demonstrated its inability to recognize other identities, work with them, and bring about their integration into French society. All of these factors should be taken into account; nevertheless, the

November riots and the social tensions they revealed must not be reduced to questions of multiculturalism or religion alone. Rather, it is the overlap of these issues with the social question that creates its complexity.

Periods of protest, especially when they take violent forms, tend to give a unified picture of the participants. So it was for the riots in November 2005, which were interpreted not only as a violent response to the death of two young people and the insulting comments of a government minister, but also as a general expression of the exclusion and disqualification that youth in these underprivileged areas feel. To understand these events, we must take into account numerous factors. Not all underprivileged areas were affected by the riots; many young people not living in social housing and less affected by racial discrimination were not heavily involved. These riots were indeed the expression of exclusion and a profound resentment that brought into play both ethnoracial (youth of African immigrant background, directly affected by discrimination and racism) and social dimensions (youth of low-income background). Emphasizing these aspects does not mean denying the increasing precariousness of young people in general or neglecting the growing intergenerational employment inequalities and lack of upward social mobility. Rather, it allows us to show that the riots did not develop simply on the basis of age and class; they also brought into play the urban forms of the increasing precariousness of part of the low-income population—particularly those of immigrant origin.

The protest movement in response to the CPE revealed this same tension between two main elements: a general reaction to a government plan perceived to reinforce the fragility and precariousness of working conditions for young people and internal stratification stemming from social and educational inequalities during the long period between adolescence and employment on the other. This is exacerbated by the fact that the French school system, in terms of recruiting students and the importance of having a degree in finding a job, pits prestigious universities (the famous *grandes écoles*) against nonselective mass universities.[11]

## Comparing the riots to the student movement

The occurrence of two large mobilizations of French youth in a short period of time allows us not only to highlight the fundamental differences at the heart of the two respective groups, which reveals two different forms of collective action; it also allows us to identify the factors and dynamics at work in each case.

Although the riots and the student movement were two proximate events involving young people, they were not connected. The anti-CPE movement did not position itself in relation to the riots; it neither supported nor condemned them. Rather, the anti-CPE movement was formed in response to a government reform that was perceived as worsening the insecurity of young college graduates. This student mobilization took place independent of the riots that had occurred only a few months before in numerous working-class neighborhoods. Although the general trend of making the youth workforce more flexible appeared to be a motivating factor in both cases, this trend did not produce united action.

The dimensions indicated in Figure 4.1 point to the greater complexity of the riots relative to the anti-CPE student movement. In effect, the events of November 2005 cannot be reduced to a single dimension, whether it is social, ethnic, spatial, or political. Rather, it is the intermingling of all of the factors in the figure that explains much of the intensity of the riots, along with their territorial diffusion, their weak politicization, and the profile of the youth involved. By comparison, the anti-CPE movement appears to be a classic student protest, similar in form and demands to the protests against various government legislation proposed between 1980 and 1990.[12]

Above all, Figure 4.1 shows that a single dimension can play an important role in both contexts while having different content. Moreover, we see that it is possible for some factors that are important in one case to play only a minor role in the other. This is especially true for the ethnoracial and spatial aspects, which played decisive roles in the riots but were of secondary importance in the structuring of the student movement.

NEW DIRECTIONS FOR YOUTH DEVELOPMENT • DOI: 10.1002/yd

# Figure 4.1. Comparison of Riots and Student Movement Sociological Framework

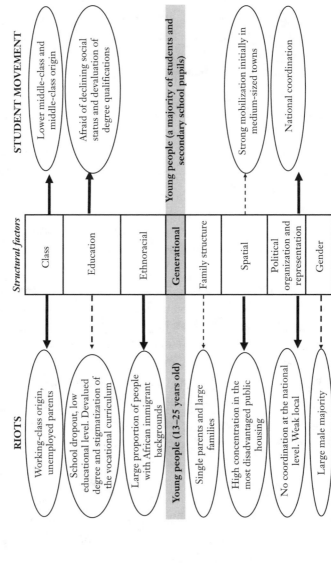

*Note:* The figure shows which social dimensions were important in structuring and explaining the two social movements: the thicker and more solid the arrow, the more important the factor.

Besides the universally important generational aspect, only two dimensions, social background and political organization/representation, played a deciding role in both movements. However, they differed radically in their content. Most of the youth in the riots were of working-class background, with parents who were either unemployed or receiving minimum income support. By contrast, most of the youth who mobilized against the CPE were from the stable minority of the working class or the lower middle class.

As for the political dimensions, the differences between the two events clearly reveal the difficulty that the political and trade union systems have in representing the interests and expectations of young people living in working-class areas.[13] From the beginning, the student mobilization was able to profit from the involvement of political parties and trade unions, whose positions radicalized, whereas it was reserve, hesitation, and suspicion that characterized their reaction to the riots. Especially in the communities that were most affected by the riots, political representatives on both the right and the left were heavily involved, often supported by networks of associations and spontaneous local demonstrations. At the national level, in addition to the police response orchestrated by the minister of the interior, the engagement of the political parties and trades union remained moderate in relation to the scope and duration of the riots. Few overall interpretations proposed by major politicians have sought to make political sense of the riots or to interpret differently the revolt of the underprivileged youth who live in areas of exclusion. In this sense, the political response to the riots was mostly repressive and penal.

The difference is clear when we compare the quick political response in support of the students. Certainly this group of young people has been politicized for quite some time. This is especially true in France where, despite a continuing drop in electoral participation, the student union remains a structuring element of university political life. It is an easily accessible resource in the event of a social movement, and its public demonstrations always have numerous implications for the political and national trade union systems.

NEW DIRECTIONS FOR YOUTH DEVELOPMENT • DOI: 10.1002/yd

The ethnoracial and specific working-class and precarious neigh-borhoods, which were of minimal importance in the student mobi-lization, played a determining role in the riots, thus accounting for many of its characteristics. The first factor, the ethnoracial dimen-sions, intervened in two ways. First, it served as a way for the youth to explain the behavior of the police toward the adolescents they were pursuing, who ended up entering an electricity substation and dying of burns they sustained there. Numerous authors have shown how the relationship between youth in working-class areas and the police has deteriorated over the past twenty years. They have also shown how this relationship is increasingly based on physical con-frontation and provocation in which the recourse to violence becomes trivialized. The strong presence of youth of immigrant background contributes heavily to the "ethnicization" of police inter-vention, which these young people experience as racial profiling—making these North African or black African youth the target of choice for law enforcement agents. Thus, the death of the adoles-cents was interpreted as the dramatic consequence of ethnoracial dis-crimination, a recurrent theme in the lives of youth of immigrant background. The explosion of violence that followed the reports of their death reflected the resentment of working-class youth who share the experience of ethnoracial stigmatization.

The ethnoracial dimension also intervened because a significant number of the youth who were directly involved in the riots were of immigrant background. Moreover, this element led certain com-mentators and the mass media (principally foreign) to present the events of November 2005 as "ethnic" riots. But if it is true that a majority of the involved youth were of immigrant background, in no instance were the actions organized on an ethnic basis, just as the violence was at no moment aimed at a specific ethnoracial group. This is a major difference with the 1992 Los Angeles riots when the violence put ethnoracial groups in opposition to each other, with territorial control playing an important role.[14] This dimension did not play the same role in the emergence and devel-opment of the student movement in France, although it did mani-fest itself during certain incidents toward the end of the protests, when small and isolated groups of nonstudents (a majority of them black) attacked some protesters.[15] These events, which contributed to the attacks and the looting that took place during the protests, sowed discord in the university and high school students without ever making the ethnoracial difference a dividing line.

The spatial dimension is easier to analyze by comparing the two events because it is woven intimately into the diffusion of the riots, whereas it appears marginal in the other case. The geography of the riots clearly demonstrates which neighborhoods were involved: a majority of the areas affected were among the most working-class and precarious neighborhoods, with a strong presence of immigrants or people of immigrant background. These neighborhoods are also considered "problematic" by urban policy, which tends to develop specific policies focused only on these areas, and deteriorating public housing in these areas is common. We will see in the following section how the segregation in these neighborhoods has contributed to transforming the concept of the social world from one that is thought of in terms of inequality to one that is conceived in terms of discrimination. Stigmatization and segregation have contributed to the consolidation of a "community of destinies" (that is, one of pariahs) among young people. The territorial dimension also played a determining role because the most intense conflicts with the police, as well as the most flagrant civil rights abuses, have taken place either inside or at the edges of public housing projects. Intimate knowledge of these spaces gave a strategic advantage to the youth, who were operating on terrain that was difficult for the police to control. The urban guerrilla warfare quality of some of the violence is explained by the configuration of these large public housing projects, which are difficult for outsiders to penetrate and control.

Territorial aspects were of only secondary importance for the student movement. Just as with other mobilizations during the 1990s, middle-sized provincial university towns were often the first to mobilize on a large scale, with the size and influence of the local student body being conducive to this type of demonstration. These are also the mass universities where student uncertainty as to the value of their education is high.[16]

Finally, two dimensions that are represented by dashed lines in Figure 4.1 in the case of the riots (family structure and gender) are absent in the anti-CPE student movement. There are two reasons that they are dashed rather than solid lines. The few facts available and the observations made at the time of the riots clearly show that a majority of the rioters were young men; the charges that were filed and information obtained during police interviews confirm this. However, little research has been undertaken to examine this question, even if classic explanations could help explain why these young men's most intense involvement was in violent actions against the police.

## Segregation and discrimination

From the 1990s onward, discrimination has been a major issue in the political and institutional arenas, in common discourse, and in the social sciences. This process has been accompanied by the creation of such institutions as the High Authority for the Fight Against Discrimination and for Equality (la HALDE).[17] Although this organization aims to counteract all forms of discrimination, it pays special attention to offenses of an ethnic or racial character due to the tendency of French society not to give them high priority and not to devote enough resources to recording them statistically and combating them legally. Far more than just a realization of the need to identify, measure, and eliminate ethnoracial discrimination, this trend refers to the transition from an idea of society conceived in terms of class and social inequality to one founded on the dimensions of ethnicity and discrimination.

While numerous sociologists have pointed out this process, not many have identified the importance of segregation in their analyses. This has helped reinforce the paradigm of the transition mentioned above: the shift toward a society in which ethnocultural (ethnoracial) identities and the discrimination they imply take precedence. Unequal access to housing, employment, and health care, as well as unequal treatment by the police and in jails, thus tends to be analyzed primarily in terms of ethnic or racial discrimination.

NEW DIRECTIONS FOR YOUTH DEVELOPMENT • DOI: 10.1002/yd

If the link between segregation and discrimination appears to be particularly tenuous for this socio-urban configuration, it must not be reduced to the ethnoracial dimension. It is necessary to identify the nature of this link and its dynamics. This allows us to understand how urban segregation acts on school segregation not only in quantitative terms (for example, the highest concentration of underprivileged students) but also in qualitative terms, that is, the academic difficulties of these students stem from deliberately discriminatory treatment by the academic establishment.[18] Thus, youth themselves view discrimination, not their own shortcomings, as the reason for their academic difficulties.[19]

Such logic reappears when we consider the difficulties that youth in these areas have in finding jobs.[20] Little sociological work has focused on the custom of denouncing discrimination as a way of masking one's own dysfunctions or maladjustments (at work, at school, and so on) by diverting them to social determinations (such as unacknowledged or bottled-up inequality, for example).

This way of thinking implies that we must first distinguish inequality from discrimination.[21] We will thus speak of inequality as the result of an unintentional structural process that translates into unequal access to resources and social positions according to classic sociological factors such as social origin, level of education, ethnoracial dimensions, location of residence, age, gender, and family structure. By contrast, discrimination refers to an intentional process of differentiated and unfavorable treatment of an individual or a group based on one or several characteristics. The intent of this unfavorable treatment is perceived as such by individuals who are affected by it. This point is complex and important because inequality can result from a deliberate process of shunting aside certain groups without necessarily aiming for them to be treated in an unfavorable manner. This process reveals what is commonly referred to as "perverse effects" in sociology, a phrase used to describe an action with unintended consequences. In some cases, the outcome may even be contrary to the actor's intentions. For example, parents may very well want to avoid places where there is a preponderance of children of immigrant origin, without, however, seeking to treat such people unfavorably in terms of educational access or the quality of the education. Neither the protagonists of this "avoidance" nor the people stigmatized by it perceive such behavior as discrimination. What is important in the definition posited here is the individual's subjective perception of a situation that he or she will interpret as the result of a deliberate action seeking to accord to him or her unfavorable treatment on the basis of one or several characteristics. If stigmatization often implies discrimination, the link is neither mechanical nor systematic.

Thus, discrimination contains a profound subjective dimension. However, pronounced inequality is not necessarily interpreted in terms of discrimination, just as real discrimination is not necessarily perceived as such by those concerned. It is indeed the combination of these two aspects—their intentional character and the perception of this intentionality by those who are affected—that generally constitutes the point of departure for revolts or large-scale mobilizations, especially when discrimination disregards the laws and rules currently in force.

With reference to the disintegration approach, we can say that urban segregation plays a role on three levels.[22] First, on the social-structural level, it limits access to labor and consumer markets, which weakens occupational and social position. Second, on the institutional level (at least in the French case), it reduces opportunities to participate in decision-making processes and to access political resources. Finally, on the personal level, urban segregation contributes to lowered self-esteem, as well as the recognition and acceptance of personal and group identities by other groups—because of stigmatization and spatial exclusion. The main result is to damage such recognition, a favorable element among young people for explaining the use of violence and interpreting their own situation in terms of discrimination.

Figure 4.2 lays out the scope of this analysis. The analytical dimensions I have identified (social origin, level of education, ethnicity/race, location of residence, age, gender, family structure) correspond to the domains that are typically linked to the production of inequality. They all played a role in the structuring and development of the riots.

Figure 4.2. The Impact of Segregation on Inequalities and Discrimination

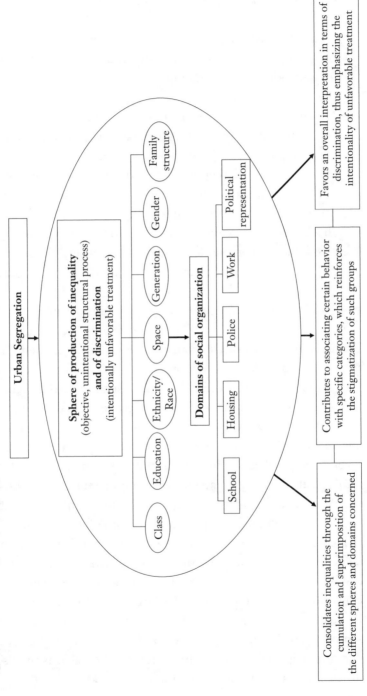

However, two factors merit special consideration:

1. These dimensions do not necessarily act on the production of inequality with the same intensity or according to the same logic. In addition, their multiple combinations give rise to complex interpretations.
2. Depending on the category in question (education, housing, security, employment, political representation), each dimension will have varying structural effects on social inequality. Consequently, the extent to which they are perceived as discrimination will differ. In other words, certain factors are more linked to an interpretation in terms of inequality, while others are more linked to an interpretation in terms of discrimination. For example, social class is more commonly associated with inequality than with discrimination, whereas the inverse is true for ethnicity and gender.

Examining a few examples will help explain this dynamic.

For quite some time, sociologists have highlighted educational inequality linked to social origin.[23] The social actors themselves most often perceive this situation as the result of an unintentional process on the part of individuals or institutions; they tend to attribute it to the unequal distribution of economic and cultural capital, which manifests itself as disproportionate access to knowledge and an unequal relationship with the modes of academic evaluation. Their feeling is that it is not a deliberate intention of the institution or of specific groups to discriminate against people on the basis of social class in granting them access to higher education. Thus, they do not make an initial interpretation in terms of discrimination.

However, in areas such as law enforcement, housing, and employment, ethnoracial discrimination appears to be determinant and is often experienced as such. Everyday experiences with racism contribute to their construction as discrimination rather than as inequality and bring to the fore ethnoracial aspects as the main source of discrimination. Sources linked to social background, gender, and neighborhood are thus diluted, whereas it is precisely urban segregation in the most disadvantaged areas that produces an interweaving of all these factors and can amplify discrimination. In effect, those that are linked to the ethnoracial dimensions are also intimately linked to those referring to other criteria, such as age, gender, and where one lives.

In this way, we better understand how each dimension acts differently on various areas of society. Urban segregation in disadvantaged working-class areas is at the very heart of this process, acting in three ways. First, it reinforces the association and intermingling of dimensions (such as class, ethnicity/race, age, gender, neighborhood, and so on) that are less spontaneously correlated in instances during which there is less segregation based on these elements.[24]

Second, it tends to associate some situations and behaviors with certain social categories and specific ethnic groups to such an extent that these characteristics become identified with these groups, which end up being perceived and defined in reference to these phenomena. In this way, a significant number of youth of immigrant background in a school is most likely to be perceived as a factor of disorder, or as reducing the quality of academic instruction, just as their presence in a public place will be perceived as a potential factor of insecurity. To the extent that the segregated groups in these neighborhoods are already the most stigmatized, the visibility of their concentration reinforces this stigmatization and a homogenized vision of such groups. This is how violence, delinquency, incivility, academic failure, and so on are less related to the social contexts that generate them than they are to the stigmatized groups themselves.

Finally, it favors the transition from the logic of inequality to the logic of discrimination; in other words, it tends to transform a person's outlook on society and on his or her own situation from a perception that is conceived in terms of inequality to one that is thought of in terms of discrimination. It is not a black-or-white question, but rather a gradual shift that does not completely erase the vision conceived in terms of inequality.

This transformation is particularly noticeable in education. The social and ethnic homogeneity of certain establishments, which are associated with a less diversified and less attractive curriculum, is no longer perceived as resulting from social inequality (which is more "legitimate" and therefore more easily accepted). Above all, it is perceived as the result of an intentional process of exclusion and of differentiated, unfavorable treatment based on characteristics of which the strong spatial concentration amplifies the stigmatization and visibility.[25] This works in favor of the dissemination of the logic of discrimination, which is traditionally associated with certain dimensions (mainly ethnicity/race and gender) and with certain domains (law enforcement, housing, and employment), to the entire society.[26] This includes school, whose decisions and evaluations appear to be increasingly perceived as discrimination.

Areas that have a strong presence of working-class citizens and immigrants from North and sub-Saharan Africa provide a good example of this dual process. The multiple factors that produce inequality in these areas are heavily interwoven. The image of a young man who is poorly educated, of working-class and immigrant background, and living in a housing project embodies these consolidated characteristics that reinforce their own capacity to amplify inequality and promote their perception as discrimination. They cannot, however, be reduced to ethnoracial aspects. In this way, young men in these areas perceive actions taken by police as discriminatory actions based on these young men's identification not only with a certain ethnoracial group, but also with a neighborhood, a gender, and a social class.[27] In this context, urban segregation contributes to the transformation of a personal experience into collective experience.

From Figure 4.2, we understand that the French riots were not an ethnic conflict. Certainly the experience of ethnic and racial discrimination was a crucial aspect in producing hatred and deep resentment, but the revolt was never a clash between ethnic groups, and the movement was not organized on the basis of specific ethnic interests. It also was not only a class revolt. Segregation was the element that created the context for the riots by transforming inequalities into visible and intolerable discrimination. More than a wish stemming from ethnic self-organization or community division, it could be interpreted as a strong request for state intervention in order to reclaim dignity and achieve equal opportunities. It also raised the question of political representation for working people of African immigrant background living in depressed areas. The French national and local political system has challenges ahead in facing this situation.

## Notes

1. According to this legislation, employees under the age of twenty-six can be dismissed from their job during the first two years of their employment without a reason given.

2. Belaïd, C. (Ed.). (2006). *Banlieue, lendemain de révolte.* Paris: La Dispute; Kokoreff, M., Osganian, P., & Simon, P. (2006). Emeutes et après? *Mouvements, 44,* 9–120; Mucchielli, L., & Le Goaziou, V. (Eds.). (2006). *Quand les banlieues brûlent . . . Retour sur les émeutes de novembre 2005.* Paris: La Découverte.

3. Anhut, R., & Heitmeyer, W. (2000). *Disintegration, recognition and violence.* http://a.dorna.free.fr/RevueNo9/Rubrique2/R2SR1.htm.

4. Based on a sociological approach, this article focuses on the structural dimensions of the riots, the socio-economic and socio-political factors that have an impact in producing specific collective behaviours and representations. For this reason, it does not deal with socioemotional and psychological dimensions, another important issue that is often neglected too.

5. This section takes up again arguments presented in Lagrange, H., & Oberti, M. (Eds.) (2006). *Emeutes urbaines et protestations. Une singularité française.* Paris: Presses de Sciences Po.

6. Lapeyronnie, D. (1993). *L'individu et les minorités.* Paris: PUF; Schnapper, D. (2007). *Qu'est-ce que l'intégration?* Paris: Gallimard.

7. Castel, R. (1995). *Les métamorphoses de la question sociale.* Paris: Fayard; Chauvel, L. (2002). *Le destin des générations.* Paris: PUF; Noiriel, G. (2006). *Le creuset français. Histoire de l'immigration XIX°-XX° siècle.* Paris: Editions du Seuil.

8. Petonnet, C. (1979). *On est tous dans le brouillard: Ethnologie des banlieues.* Paris: Éditions Galilée; Sayad, A. (1999). *La double absence: Des illusions de l'émigré aux souffrances de l'immigré.* Paris: Le Seuil; Segalen, M. (1990). *Nanterriens, les familles dans la ville: Une ethnologie de l'identité.* Toulouse: Presses universitaires du Mirail.

9. Kakpo, N. (2007). *L'Islam, un recours pour les jeunes.* Paris: Presses de Sciences Po.

10. The Los Angeles riots started after the court acquittal of police officers who had been videotaped beating a black man. During six days of rioting, thousands of people were involved in widespread looting and assault. Fifty-three people died, and about two thousand were injured.

11. Bourdieu, P. (1989). *La noblesse d'etat.* Paris: Editions de Minuit.

12. Galland, O., & Oberti, M. (1996). *Les étudiants.* Paris: La Découverte, coll. Repères.

13. Masclet, O. (2003). *La gauche et les cités.* Paris: La Dispute.

14. Bergesen, A., & Herman, M. (1998). Immigration, race, and riot: The 1992 Los Angeles uprising. *American Sociological Review, 63,* 39–54.

15. Bronner, L. (2006, March 25). Au coeur d'une bande du "9–3," le plaisir de la violence. *Le Monde*.

16. Beaud, S. (2002). 80% au "bac" *et après?: les enfants de la démocratisation scolaire*. Paris: Ed. La Découverte; Duru-Bellat, M. (2006). *L'inflation scolaire. Les désillusions de la méritocratie*. Paris: Le Seuil.

17. La Haute Autorité de Lutte contre les Discriminations et pour l'Égalité (HALDE) is an administrative authority created in December 2004: "Our general mission is as follows: to combat discrimination as prohibited by law; to provide all necessary information; to assist victims; and to identify and promote just practices in order to reinforce the principle of equality. We retain the legal right to conduct investigations concerning such matters." http://www.halde.fr.

18. See Oberti, M. (2007). *L'école dans la ville: Ségrégation, mixité et carte scolaire*. Paris: Presses de Sciences Po.

19. This marks an evolution from what François Dubet highlighted in his work on "the hassle" (*la galère*), in which he demonstrated how some youth living in public housing attributed the difficulties they had at school or in integrating themselves into society to "personal" weaknesses or shortcomings. Dubet, F. (1987). *La galère*. Paris: Fayard.

20. Kakpo. (2007).

21. Schnapper, D. Lutte contre les discriminations et lien social. In S. Paugam (Ed.), *Repenser la solidarité* (pp. 515–529). Paris: PUF, 2007.

22. Anhut & Heitmeyer. (2000).

23. Duru-Bellat, M. (2002). *Les inégalités sociales à l'école. Genèses et mythes*. Paris: PUF.

24. This has already been revealed by Dominique Duprez (1997): Entre discrimination et désaffiliation: L'expérience des jeunes issus de l'immigration maghrébine. *Les Annales de la recherche urbaine*, 76, 79–88.

25. This is why urban segregation contributes to the dilution of the effects of each factor, acting simultaneously as an objective element and subjective dimension of discrimination. Comparative studies in areas that sharply contrast with each other with respect to their social and urban profiles would allow us to better understand the experience of discrimination according to the level and type of segregation, as well as the way in which discrimination is associated with certain factors.

26. This has played a large role in explaining the scope of France's November 2005 urban riots. See Lagrange, H., & Oberti, M. (Eds.). (2006). *Émeutes urbaines et protestations. Une singularité française*. Paris: Presses de Sciences Po.

27. Some rap lyrics covering the theme of the ghetto demonstrate the multidimensional aspect of the perception of discrimination and its effects on the amplification of rage.

MARCO OBERTI *is an associate professor at Sciences Po Paris and a research fellow at the Observatoire sociologique du Changement.*

*Young people are active and rational agents who can contribute to an understanding of society and their own behavior. This article examines English society's fears of youth violence and antisocial behavior.*

# 5

# Fears of violence among English young people: Disintegration theory and British social policy

*Tom Cockburn*

THIS ARTICLE EXPLORES young people's fears of violence amid the backdrop of recent debates in the United Kingdom surrounding youth crime and wider debates around youth policies and social cohesion. It examines the nature of social disintegration in the north of England and the social consequences of social changes at the beginning of the twenty-first century. It focuses on the experiences of young people who are the subject of a number of social policies concerning antisocial behavior.

Unsurprisingly, young people's experiences of social disintegration are more complex than is generally considered. This article looks at how young people's experiences contribute to the disintegration theories that form the focus of this volume. Disintegration theory correctly focuses on aspects of respect and the mutual recognition of individuals and groups. The article addresses antisocial behavior, much of which is not necessarily applicable to violence; however, fears of violence underlie many of its uses.

NEW DIRECTIONS FOR YOUTH DEVELOPMENT, NO. 119, FALL 2008 © WILEY PERIODICALS, INC.
Published online in Wiley InterScience (www.interscience.wiley.com) • DOI: 10.1002/yd.274

A great deal has been written about violence in England, and this fear has prompted a number of government initiatives around law and order. Much of the attention has focused on the "respect" action plan and the introduction of acceptable behavior contracts,[1] penalty notices,[2] antisocial behavior orders (ASBOs), and dispersal orders.[3] The thrust of these initiatives is to "minimise bureaucracy and free up time of police and courts" or "claim back public spaces for the community. They have a broad populist makeup and are largely targeted at young people.

These initiatives are not without their critics. They are criticized for criminalizing young people (approximately half of ASBOs are breached, resulting in a criminal conviction) and being disproportionately used against minority ethnic and mentally ill young people.[4] The thrust of the antisocial behavior legislation has been criticized for avoiding the due process of the English legal system, including the Council of Europe, which observes they are undertaken against young people "without necessarily having committed a recognisable criminal offence."[5] It also needs noting that recent research on youth explores and takes seriously young people's perspective far more than policymakers seem to allow.[6]

## Fear of violence

Antisocial behavior initiatives have been initiated with considerable public support. The 2004/2005 British Crime Survey found that over 30 percent of respondents expressed some fear about threats from violence, with 11 percent of these expressing that they were "very worried" about physical violence.[7] This 11 percent figure rose to 22 percent of those sixteen to twenty-four years old who were "very worried" about violent crime. Young people are the most fearful of violent crime, along with those who live in high-crime areas and those from ethnic minorities. This fear probably reflects the higher likelihood that young people are victims of violent crime.[8] Thus, young people's fears can be considered rational. Most of the literature around being a victim of crime has shown that the concept of being at risk is more complex than at first imagined.[9] Individual predictions of risk are largely based on interpretations far removed from rational considerations of likelihood based on recorded crime rates. However, a closer focus on young people and ethnic minorities, and their greater risks of being victims of crime, shows a clearer level of rationality and realistic calculation. Young people do not report most incidents of violence for fear of reprisals, or they believe that violent behavior is normal and in general are not happy with the way perpetrators of violence are dealt with by adults, whether in school or by the criminal justice system.

Fear of crime has been the target of politicians and the popular press, and the rhetoric and policy implications have resulted in legislation that seeks to adopt an increasingly punitive model of justice on behalf of victims. Yet as Williams has argued, the use of severe punishments for offenders has been at the expense of restorative programs that have a more successful record.[10]

## Disintegration theory

A variety of theories seek to explain violence, and the focus of this volume is on disintegration theory, which has synthesized a number of approaches. From the perspective of disintegration theory, "disintegration marks the failure of social institutions and communities to deliver existential basics, social recognition and personal integrity."[11] The theory is applied to a number of conflicting groups in modern societies, but it is particularly apposite in terms of how societies view young people. It has resonance with specific groups of young people within societies who tend to be the object of criminal justice policies. In many respects, our social institutions and communities have failed to deliver the existential basics and offer the social recognition that allows many young people to feel respected and valued. Indeed, the danger of many of the policies identified at the beginning of this article is that they will exacerbate these problems.

In order to explore this topic further, it is necessary to break down the processes of recognition and social integration that Anhut and Heitmeyer outlined, where a successful balance in the relationship between an individual's freedom and attachment assumes importance. Crucially, social disintegration occurs when the equilibrium of these balances is disturbed. This occurs on three levels. The first level is the overall structural level of participation in the material and cultural goods of society. On a structural level, individuals need to participate in labor markets, live in adequate housing, and be able to enjoy a certain level of consumption. Clearly there will be inequalities in the distribution of these scarce resources, but the key to an integrated society is for individuals to be subjectively happy with their social position. Young people will, with very few exceptions, be in a weak position in relation to the labor market, housing, and consumer power. After all, they are starting their working careers and are still dependent on family housing. As we will see, it is when the transitions to full adulthood go wrong that social disintegration occurs for many young people.

The second level identified by disintegration theorists is that of institutional socialization toward democratic principles, where people view themselves and others as of equal moral status. Participation in modern democratic societies is premised on a plurality of conflicting groups. Different groups have different interests, and resolving these interests peacefully will occur only if all parties can perceive fairness and justice. Perceptions of fairness and justice are subjective, however, and some young people do not see themselves as fairly and equally treated.

The third level involves a personal (communicative) establishment of emotional and expressive relations between people in order to make sense of themselves and others. Here it is important to have space for people to develop their sense of self-esteem and identity in accordance with wider normative values. Clearly, young people are in a very early stage of adjusting to this and must be given the space to make mistakes, without these mistakes becoming the primary way they are defined (for example, as violent, criminal, or deviant).

NEW DIRECTIONS FOR YOUTH DEVELOPMENT • DOI: 10.1002/yd

## Social disintegration in the north of England

The former mill and mining towns of the north of England are typically characterized as being blighted by high levels of feral unemployed young people alienated from the labor market and citizenship. The region reflects the decline from the nineteenth-century mills and mines to its attempts to regenerate its economic base in a highly competitive national and international context.[12] Nevertheless, youth unemployment here is relatively low, and youth unemployment in the north of England is not as acute as in other parts of Europe. The preoccupation with issues of unemployment has led some writers in the youth field to suggest that other aspects of young people's vulnerability have been overlooked.[13] Within the category of the unemployed is a host of subcategories that have very different needs, such as young people who have caring responsibilities to members of their family, those with disabilities and poor health, and those with a history of alienation and disaffection. A focus on the unemployed also masks the difficulties that many young people in employment experience, such as low pay, job insecurity, and poor training.

The challenge of global markets with workforce requirements based on technological change and new communication systems have stimulated U.K. government policies that have eroded workforce protection from competition and undermined traditional community structures in British towns and cities. In this sense, British cities are to provide, as Alam and Husband have argued, "the spatial concentration and clustering of essential competitive assets."[14] Thus, urban environments are placed in a context characterized by insecurity, low pay, short-term contracts, and high competition. Far from communities' closing ranks against international competition, the competitiveness has turned within and between urban communities. The bulk of suspicion has been turned toward perceived outsiders, such as economic migrants and asylum seekers. In the summer of 2001, for example, civil disturbances took place in several northern English towns (Burnley, Bradford, Oldham, Leeds, and Stoke-on-Trent). These disturbances generated a plethora of government reports, centering on issues of social cohesion and the interactions between racial groups, highlighting relationships between young people (especially young men) from different ethnic communities. It is worth noting how British government policy has replaced a commitment to equality to one based on individual opportunity where all have an equal chance to succeed.

## Solidarity versus individuality

Disintegration theorists have focused on the way that principles of moral equality and solidarity work in tension with a complementary and contrasting principle of individualization. The tensions of these principles have been explored in relation to criminality in the European context.[15] The task falls on the government and education system to instill values. However, those of moral equality and solidarity are dwarfed by those based on individualism and competition.

Much of the concern since the 1990s has centered on the perceived political and social apathy of young people and the wish to turn them into active citizens. Young people are reluctant to vote and participate in traditional institutions and often feel unsafe on the streets, in school, and even in their home. However, a core of young people are quite committed, and when the question asks young people what they intend to do, the vast majority of young people in the United Kingdom declare themselves to be interested in politics.[16] Lemos and Bacon have noted that for young people, domestic politics seems dry, empty, and irrelevant, but they are concerned about their own communities and what is happening internationally.[17]

Young people are prepared for social, civic, and political life in public institutions that are not democratically run; as Lerner said: "For the most part, young people's days are spent in a few major systems; schools, juvenile justice systems. . . . In general, these systems are non-responsive to a civic way of being—to democratic practice. Therefore, if we are serious about youth civic engagement, the challenge . . . includes finding ways to address the structural impediments."[18] These structural impediments include institutions that are geared up to placing young people in a competitive labor market rather than promoting civic engagement and political respect. One United Nations special rapporteur expressed concern with the way citizenship education in the United Kingdom is not linked to children's rights. Rights are, she says, "perceived as different from and alien to the rights and freedoms that learners will recognise in the everyday lives."[19] The rapporteur also noted that individualism and competitiveness (fostered by exam success and competition between schools for successful assessment results) clashed with solidarity and community. Indeed, as Lemos and Bacon have commented, few government policies are geared toward turning young people into good citizens; more seem to be designed to restrain and punish them for bad behavior.[20]

Much of the social commentary on young people in the United Kingdom perceives them as either a risk or at risk. These characterizations pay little attention to the emotional and expressive side of young people's lives. Young people are processed through a competitive education and find themselves in an equally competitive labor market. The expectation is for poorer young people to feel disempowered, disengaged, excluded, or victimized or, in the words of one influential U.K. report, that "freedom's orphans" "are on the verge of mental breakdown, at risk from antisocial behaviour, self-harm, drug and alcohol abuse."[21] While this characterizes some young people's identities in the United Kingdom, the surprise perhaps is that most young people do feel connected to their place, heritage, and identity. Young people do have a sense of expressive and emotional relations between people, and this is linked to their communities. The importance of place and space remains important in a world where labor mobility is assumed.

Understanding the importance of social identities has a relatively long history in academia. Social identities are closely connected with ethnicities that are seen as natural and constant in the complexity of modern societies. Stuart Hall has written about how identities of "Englishness" are culturally constructed as "a particularly closed, exclusive and regressive form of English national identity."[22] Despite the heterogeneity of ethnic communities in British urban environments, Englishness is constructed "only by marginalizing, dispossessing, displacing and forgetting other ethnicities."[23] This exclusiveness can, at times of crisis or dislocation, lead to intercommunal violence.[24]

## Reconceptualizing the "problem of youth"

Disintegration theory correctly directs academic focus to the recognition deficits an individual may experience in life.[25] That is, individuals may react destructively to prior injuries to their social recognition and self-respect. Anhut and Heitmeyer have identified some moderating variables: social competence, whereby individuals who are equipped with social competencies are better able to cope with their surroundings; patterns of accountability, whereby people allocate responsibility toward perceived failures in their lives; and social comparison processes, which relativize a person's own sense of recognition amid others.[26] All of these are helpful concepts in understanding young people's fears and acts of violence, but in my view, they need to be sensitive to the ways social problems occur in local contexts and the ways in which social competencies are prescribed.

For children and young people, the relationship of psychological symbiosis usually works in a negative way in their relationships with adults. Their competence is undermined almost constantly, and their actions are represented in demeaning ways that serve to denigrate young people's contributions and constantly question their competence. The implications of redefining young people's competence have far-reaching consequences. In youth policy literature, the "problem" of youth may be due not to an unsuitable legislative framework or the behavior of young people themselves, but to the extent to which society is able to be inclusive and respectful of young people. Currently, this seems to be dominated by adults' reluctance to give ground to minors.

It is therefore necessary to reevaluate how young people are placed within policy initiatives. In England, young people have been consistent and major losers. For instance, the establishment of neighborhood watch schemes, community safety liaison panels, and those given prominence in representing communities have been dominated by people in their fifties and sixties, who tend to relay commonly held fears of children and young people.

Smithson and Flint, in their study of how antisocial behavior policies have been operationalized in a small district of Manchester, noted that the new powers led to an increase in reporting of antisocial behavior by residents, which itself led to a serious disintegration in young people's relationships with the police and other professionals who wished to work with them. The introduction of dispersal orders in the area coincided with the earlier closing of a youth center at 9:00 P.M. The area saw an increasing fear of young people and disintegrated young people's relationships with most adults in the community.[27] It could be argued that the strained relations with adults and professionals served to increase young people's recognition-deficit status. Disintegration theorists are correct to point out that aggression may become manifest and "can only be conceivable as a *relational* connection."[28]

## *Young people's views of public spaces*

Young people are often seen as the cause of urban crime and decay. In a world of shifting boundaries of the body, gender roles, ethnicity, and other characteristics, there is "increasing anger at children who cannot or will not fulfil their expected roles in the transmission of 'traditional values.'"[29] Thus, young people are presented "as malicious predators, the embodiment of dangerous natural forces, unharnessed to social ends."[30] This can be seen in the response to social exclusion where young people are associated with persistent young offenders, rowdyism, and vandalism. We need to pay attention to the contextually specific questions of the social, political, and discursively created ways young people are described, analyzed, and theorized by academics, local communities, and nation builders. The important question to ask is how young people themselves see public spaces.

## Perceptions of danger

This section presents a selection of voices of young people gained from a number of projects I have undertaken in two towns and three cities in the north of England in the past three years. I do not attempt to provide any empirical generalization but to provide illustrations as to how adult assumptions about young people are at times erroneous, how government policies may exacerbate the dangers young people experience, and how any theoretical synthesis must engage with young people's views rather than relying on the perspective of adults. The section is broken into two sections outlining young people's perceptions of danger and the strategies used by young people to remain safe.

There is a plethora of research exploring perceptions of fear and danger throughout the Western world. Most of this work consists of survey data or analysis of secondary data. Few reports undertake qualitative work with young people exploring the issue of danger and victimhood.

Despite the negative image of urban environments held by outsiders, these places remain spaces where young people enjoy living. The abundance of research, reports, inquiries, and commentaries highlights the social and economic deprivations of the areas and the disadvantages suffered by their citizens, and focus on the times of crisis and key events, such as riots, civil disturbances, intercommunal violence, and gang murders. It is refreshing that young people remain optimistic about these areas. One young woman comments: "I would not like to live anywhere else. I feel comfortable here. I have friends and family, and we look after each other." Another comments, "There are so many things going on around here, there are parties and great mates to hang around with."

As a middle-class researcher, my own perceptions of safety were in contrast to the young people's views of safety. A week after a high-profile gang shooting, I was surprised by a young man who felt afraid to roam too far from where he lived. He perceived dangers to exist on streets that I considered safe, in contrast to the street where another young man was violently murdered. He explained: "I know what is what here. I know I am not going to get grief from anyone. Everyone knows me and leaves me alone. If I go outside, there could be some bad people around and if I go into . . . I can get hassled by the police."

The perceptions of dangers are different for some young people. These dangers can be exacerbated by the actions of police and other security services. One young woman explained that she would go to places that are well lit and warm at night, for example, to the railway station concourse. However, she said, older male travelers would try to pick her up or make sexual innuendos that frightened her and her friends. She wanted her male friends to be near so she would feel safe. However, the security guards asked her male friends to leave because groups of young men were viewed as threatening. The station security team was not interested in the way older men bothered the young women and did nothing about it. The result was that the young women continued to be hassled, and this young woman and her friends had to leave the concourse. Thereby, the young women were exposed to further danger as they had to leave the relative safety of the railway concourse.

Visitors to urban districts across the north of England in the evenings will see young people hanging out around well-lit shopping spaces. Older residents perceive these groups as threats, and considerable tensions arise over the presence of these young people, especially young men. The new antisocial behavior powers, such as ASBOs and dispersal orders, are being used to clear young people from these spaces. But the young people like these places because they are usually located centrally, are well lit, and have a movement of people where they feel safe. Moving young people away from the shopping centers means that they then congregate outside people's houses, where residents feel threatened and are concerned by the inevitable noise associated with groups of young people. This situation serves to heighten tensions between residents and young people and also increases the chances of police involvement, thereby furthering the alienation of young people and increasing the tensions with authorities.

The movement of young people away from well-lit public spaces drives them as well to other less protected public spaces, such as parks, where other dangers may arise. As one young man put it, "Since we have been coming to the park there are loads of druggies and boozers [derogatory words for people who take drugs and drink alcohol] in there. We now sit amongst used needles and stuff. There are some really dodgy people there and we feel really frightened, especially when the lights from our mobies [cell phones] run out."[31]

This example again shows the actions of authorities pushing young people into spaces with arguably greater levels of risk and harm. Another group of young people I spoke to used to meet in a local park, which they considered safe and offered them a degree of freedom. However, when a policy of closing the park at dark was initiated, the young people felt aggrieved, and they thought it was unjust that dog walkers were still permitted to use the space at all hours.

This article is not an empirical piece, and the examples have been used to illustrate a number of points. The first is the importance of adding young people's voices to our accounts, as they can contain important details that are not seen from the perspective of adults. Second, the contrasting perceptions of adults, young people, and the authorities perhaps need to consider mediation as a first option rather than automatically assuming young people's culpability. Third, the actions of legislators and enforcers serve at times to increase the likelihood of some young citizens' becoming victims of antisocial behavior, crime, and violence. Finally, the policies at the train station and parks are enforced by private security companies. The increasing privatization of policing in the United Kingdom raises issues of public accountability and levels of training that one expects with the public police service but may not be so in the private companies.[32]

### Strategies used to remain safe

On one level, young people's behavior looks as though they are either actively seeking attention for antisocial behavior and putting themselves at risk, or they are displaying a level of stupidity and irresponsibility concerning their own safety. They gather together in the street, parks, or alleyways; they get drunk and dress in more revealing clothes.

Although I do not refute the advice that young people should necessarily avoid waiting in streets, should put on warm clothes, and certainly should steer clear of alcohol, I would like to retrieve some of the rationality behind some of the behavior. Indeed, young people have an extensive and rather sophisticated knowledge of the dangers that surround them and adopt strategies to protect themselves. In the absence or paucity of youth centers, young people are in effect forced into dangerous spaces when they are excluded from relatively safe, well-lit, and busy areas. Young people would rather stay in those spaces, but these are often denied to them.

Friday and Saturday nights in the centers of English towns and cities are usually crowded with young people enjoying a night out. Some of the young people wear few clothes for the time of year; young men and women walk about, often in the middle of winter, without a coat. When I asked a group of young women about this, I asked whether this was to show off. This was strenuously denied. One young woman explained: "No, it is not to impress lads or ought like that. It is because when we get into a club, you have to pay for the cloakroom. We are also leaving at two in the morning, and I want to show that I have nothing worth nicking [stealing], no purse, mobi, or ought (anything)." Here we can see a degree of appropriate rationality and risk management applied to a behavior that at first sight seems irrational. It would make sense to go out with nothing worth taking and be seen to have nothing because this reduces the risk of being a victim of theft or violence. Although the

young woman was aware of the subsequent danger of inappropri-
ate attention from men, she calculated that this risk was not as
likely as walking about with a coat or handbag.

Young people also displayed other calculations in their strategies to remain safe. They had a good level of local knowledge
that they could deploy. They knew which people to avoid where
and would avoid them, or they avoided places where dangerous
people would get together. While they may look irrational in
assembling on street corners, it is quite likely they are doing this
to avoid being in another place where the danger would be greater.
They would also use their knowledge of people to manage their
safety. As one young man explained, "I think it's much better to get
on the right side of [a young man with a bad reputation]. I would
go up and chat to him and talk to him. He thinks I'm okay and
leaves me and my mates alone. I know he is into drugs and the like
and has been inside [in prison] like. But I think it's better for him
to see me as a mate rather than an enemy."

Here we see that the young man understands the dangers associated with this individual with a reputation and has adopted a strategy to manage him. Although his parents would advise their son to
keep away from him, this avoidance could aggravate the situation
and place the young man in danger from his attentions.

These examples about strategies that young people use are not
uncommon. For the purposes of this article, I wish to emphasize the
importance of young people's rationality and how it may not be apparent to researchers and theorists. Appropriate methodologies need to
be adopted to capture everyone's viewpoint, as this may be important
to the sense making and explanations we are advocating. The examples here illustrate the importance of local knowledge and place.

## Conclusions and implications for disintegration theory

The conclusions that follow take young people's views seriously in
the context of where they make sense of themselves and the world
around them. As we have seen, young people are often treated as

passive and innocent objects in which their victimhood or propensity to antisocial behavior is taken for granted. In contrast to this view, it is necessary to see that active and rational people can be victims. This is not to say that quantitative studies and theoretical synthesis are less important; rather, these approaches need to engage with more qualitative empirical work with young people themselves. Second, issues that touch young people, such as violence, crime, antisocial behavior, and victimhood, are often presented in an uncritical way. We have seen how young people are presented in patronizing and passive ways, where they are seen as both a danger and in danger. But it is necessary to break through the ideological boundaries and social constructions of childhood and youth of some policymakers, researchers, and commentators. Third, some of the U.K. government's methods of dealing with violence, antisocial behavior, and crime may have led to increasing these levels by pushing young people into situations of greater risk and labeling certain groups of young people so they are more likely to meet the criminal justice system at some point. Fourth, we need to reconceptualize the "problem of youth" in ways that do not focus mostly on individual young people's choices; rather, we need to seek political and economic choices that encourage a competitive ethos in the labor market, the education system, housing, and communities that enhances social complementary rather than social comparison processes. Young people's identities are an active, creative, and complex social process that is at a crossroads. These identities are firmly located in place, memory, politics, and narrative, and sweeping generalizations and stereotypes are not appropriate.

### Notes

1. Acceptable behavior contracts are voluntary contracts made between individuals and local agencies. Over thirteen thousand were issued between 2002 and 2006.

2. Powers for police to act before court sentencing, of which 200,000 have been issued since 2004.

3. Powers for police that enable them to break up groups of young people seen as causing problems in specific areas. Eight hundred and nine dispersal orders were issued between 2004 and 2005.

    4. Thomas, T. (2007). A year of tackling anti-social behaviour: Some reflections on the realities and rhetoric. *Youth and Policy, 94,* 5–18.
    5. Council of Europe. (2005, June 8). *Report by Mr. Alvaro Gil-Robles, Commissioner for Human Rights, on his visit to the UK 4–12 November 2004.* Strasbourg: Comm DH 6.
    6. France, A. (2007). *Understanding youth in late modernity.* Buckingham: Open University Press.
    7. Allen, J. (2005). *Home Office worry about crime in England and Wales.* London: Home Office.
    8. Simmons, J., & Dodd, T. (2003). *Crime in England and Wales 2002/2003.* London: Home Office.
    9. Chadee, D., Austen, L., & Ditton, J. (2007). The relationship between likelihood and fear of criminal victimization: Evaluating risk sensitivity as a mediation concept. *British Journal of Criminology, 47,* 133–153.
    10. Williams, B. (2005). *Victims of crime and criminal justice.* London: Jessica Kingsley.
    11. Anhut, R., & Heitmeyer, W. (2006). *Disintegration, recognition and violence.* http://a.dorna.free.fr/RevueNo9/Rubrique2/R2SR1.htm
    12. Office of the Deputy Prime Minister. (2005). *State of the cities: A progress report to the delivery of sustainable communities summit.* London: Author.
    13. Furlong, A. (2006). Not a Very NEET solution: Representing problematic labour market transitions among early school-leavers. *Work, Employment and Society, 20,* 553–569.
    14. Alam, M., & Husband, C. (2006). *British Pakistani men from Bradford: Linking narratives to policy.* York: Joseph Rowntree Foundation. p. 45.
    15. Albrecht, G. (1999). Sozialer Wandel und Kriminalität. In H. J. Albrecht & H. Kury (Eds.), *Kriminalität, Strafrechtsreform und Strafvollzug in Zeiten des sozialen Umbruchs* (pp. 1–56). Freiburg: Ed. luscrim.
    16. Haste, H. (2005). *My voice, my vote, my community: A study of young people's civic action and inaction.* London: Nestle Social Research Programme.
    17. Lemos, G., & Bacon, F. (2006). *Different world: How young people can work together on human rights, citizenship, equality and creating a better society.* London: Lemos and Crane.
    18. Lerner, R. (2004). *Liberty: Thriving and civic engagement among America's youth.* London: Sage. p. 161.
    19. Tomasevski, K. (1999). *Report of the Mission on the UK, October 1999 by the Special Rapporteur on the Right to Education.* Geneva: United Nations. p. 25.
    20. Lemos & Bacon. (2006).
    21. Margo, J., Dixon, M., Pearce, N., & Reed, H. (2006). *Freedom's orphans: Raising youth in a changing world.* London: IPPR.
    22. Hall, S. (1992). The new ethnicities. In J. Donald & A. Rattansi (Eds.), *Race, culture and difference* (pp. 253–259). London: Sage. p. 256.
    23. Hall. (1992). p. 258.
    24. Heitmeyer, W. (2003). Right-wing extremist violence. In W. Heitmeyer & J. Hagen (Eds.), *International handbook on violence research.* Dordrecht: Kluwer.
    25. Albrecht, G. (2003). Sociological approaches to individual violence and their empirical evaluation. In W. Heitmeyer & J. Hagen (Ed.), *International*

*handbook of violence research* (pp. 611–656). London: Kluwer. p. 639.

26. Anhut & Heitmeyer. (2006).

27. Smithson, H., & Flint, J. (2007). Responding to young people's involvement in anti-social behaviour: A study of local initiatives in Manchester and Glasgow. *Youth and Policy, 93,* 21–39.

28. Anhut & Heitmeyer. (2006). p. 12.

29. Stephens, S. (1995). Children and the politics of culture in "late capitalism." In S. Stephens (Ed.), *Children and the politics of culture* (pp. 3–48). Princeton, NJ: Princeton University Press. p. 11.

30. Stephens. (1995). p. 13.

31. Cell phones now have lighting displays that are used as torches to provide light. However, shining the lights on cell phones drains the batteries quickly.

32. Burney, E. (2005). *Making people behave: Anti-social behaviour, politics and policy.* Devon: Willan.

TOM COCKBURN *is a lecturer in the Department of Social Sciences and Humanities, the University of Bradford, United Kingdom.*

*How can Brazilians deal with drug trafficking and its outcomes on a day-by-day basis?*

# 6

# Violence in the Brazilian *favelas* and the role of the police

*Clarissa Huguet, Ilona Szabó de Carvalho*

VIOLENCE IS PRESENT IN MANY REGIONS of the world. Among the many types of violence is structural violence, which refers to a form of violence that corresponds to the systematic ways in which a social structure or social institution kills people slowly by preventing them from meeting their basic needs. Institutionalized elitism, ethnocentricism, racism, sexism, nationalism, heterosexism, and ageism are some examples. Life spans are reduced when people are socially dominated, politically oppressed, or economically exploited. Structural violence and direct violence are highly interdependent. Structural violence inevitably produces conflict and often direct violence, including family violence, racial violence, hate crimes, terrorism, genocide, and war.

Structural violence and direct violence are highly interdependent. In this article, we analyze the relationship between the structural violence in Brazil, the armed violence in poor neighborhoods known as *favelas*, and the role of the police acting as a state agent.

Approximately 7 million people live in Rio de Janeiro, Brazil.[1] Rio de Janeiro is well known as one of the most beautiful cities in the world; however, it also holds the reputation of being one of the most violent cities in the world. Robbery, murder, and drug trafficking are

NEW DIRECTIONS FOR YOUTH DEVELOPMENT, NO. 119, FALL 2008 © WILEY PERIODICALS, INC.
Published online in Wiley InterScience (www.interscience.wiley.com) • DOI: 10.1002/yd.275

common there. In addition, juvenile crime is part of the city's reality and denotes the state's failure in helping young people in disadvantaged neighborhoods.

Rio de Janeiro is divided into two distinct worlds, known as the "asphalt"[2] and the hills.[3] According to an unofficial number, almost one million people live in the nearly seven hundred *favelas* spread across the city. Surprisingly, even for Brazilians, only a tiny percentage of this population is connected to crime and drug trafficking. Several human rights nongovernmental organizations and other reliable sources affirm that from 1 to 3 percent of this population is involved in criminality and drug trafficking.

Despite their numbers, *favela* inhabitants suffer daily prejudice and discrimination from state agents and the population in general. Although most of the *favela* residents are honest and hard-working people, the association between living in *favelas*, criminality, and the drug trafficking is extended to all poor Brazilians, in effect criminalizing poverty. This association conflates poverty with criminality, making poor Brazilians targets of inhumane treatment on a daily basis, whether as victims of drug traffickers or corrupt police agents. Furthermore, the fact that both aggressors and victims are mostly poor, undereducated black males between the ages of fifteen and twenty-four stereotypes an entire population who suffer the effects of this stigmatization.

## The emergence of the slums in Rio de Janeiro

Rio de Janeiro is not the only Brazilian city with *favelas*, but it was one of the first. The emergence of its *favelas* dates back to the end of the nineteenth century, when ex-soldiers, ex-slaves, and poor rural migrants were forced into squatter settlements due to the high land values and the enormous demand for housing. The attribution of the name *favela* seems to have several explanations. The most logical attribution stems from the *favela*, a shrub common in the northeast of Brazil where federal soldiers were fighting in a revolutionary movement aimed at keeping an autonomous community from central government control. This shrub was also found on the first hill to be occupied in Rio de Janeiro by those same soldiers, and the hill became known as Morro da Favela.[4] Today the term *favela* refers to the slums built mostly along the hillsides of Rio and other Brazilian cities.

From the start, the presence of favelas has disturbed the "civilized people" of the asphalt. The disturbance was quickly transformed into complaints directed to the public authorities. In 1927, the removal of the *favelas* was envisaged as the only solution and was included in an official project aiming to remodel Rio de Janeiro, the Brazilian capital at the time. Two years later, the first houses were built on the Morro da Rocinha.

In 1937 the *favelas* were referred to by the city as an "urban aberration," and their elimination was proposed once again. The project envisaged a prohibition on the construction of new settlements, as well as any improvements in the communities already in existence. The *favelas* were not part yet of the official city map.

In 1945 the *favelados* (those who lived in the *favelas*), afraid of the threats of removal made several times by the public authorities in Rio, reacted for the first time, formulating a list of social rights regarding the infrastructure problems they faced. In 1948, the first population census of the *favelas* was carried out. The resulting document pointed to the existence of 109 *favelas* with 138,837 inhabitants, or 7 percent of the city population. According to the document, "black and brown" people were the majority of the slums' residents due to the fact that they were "hereditarily subdeveloped, lacking ambition, and badly adjusted to the modern social demands." This explicit discrimination and marginalization of the *favelados* has hindered them since the beginning of their existence. The disorderly growth that took place just after the appearance of the slums in addition to their abandonment by the public authorities from the initial phase of the process condemned the slums and their inhabitants to marginalization and discrimination by the people of the asphalt.

In 1957 the creation of the Colligation of the Favelados Workers, whose objective was better living conditions for the inhabitants of the poor communities, strengthened the power of this social class in Rio and pressured the government to recognize their existence as citizens. At the same time, pressured by the undeniable reality of the *favelas* and the actions of its inhabitants, the Legislative Assembly allocated 3 percent of the state budget to improve the living conditions in these areas. This action was followed by a counteraction undertaken by the federal government in 1968 with the creation of the Coordination of the Habitation of Social Interest of the Metropolitan Area of RJ (Chisam). Its principal mission was to "exterminate the *favelas* of Rio de Janeiro." The Chisam defined the *favelas* as "an urban deformed space." According to Caco Barcellos in 1960, the city of Rio de Janeiro had nearly 1 million people living below the poverty line, with one-third of the population spread over 180 *favelas*.[5]

Eleven years later, in 1979, the military government created Promorar, a habitation program that based its actions on basic sanitation, transference of property titles, and other important matters. In the same year, a register of all the *favelas* of Rio was made, and a new municipal organ was created to take care of their social development and the implementation of assistance services in the *favelas*. This action was followed by several others intended to improve the miserable quality of life in the slums. The government had finally realized that it was far too late to attempt any removal within the *favelas* areas; the only feasible alternative was to try to urbanize them.

A census carried out by the Brazilian Institute of Geography and Statistics in 1991 indicated that there were approximately 962,793 people living in Rio's *favelas*. In forty-five years, the number of slum inhabitants had multiplied by seven. Faced with the indisputable truth, a habitation program designed for the poor *favela* communities, named *Favela-Bairro*, was proposed in 1993. This program, still in operation, has as its aim the construction and improvement of the main urban structure of the slums. The government, in a sharp change of approach and finally admitting that the removal of 1 million people was no longer feasible, envisaged a new status for the *favelas*: districts of the city of Rio de Janeiro.

NEW DIRECTIONS FOR YOUTH DEVELOPMENT • DOI: 10.1002/yd

Currently the Brazilian federal government is adopting a new approach and has included in its growth acceleration program the reurbanization[6] of several slums of Rio de Janeiro.

Unfortunately, criminal organizations took note of the huge gap left for decades by a negligent state that had refused to deliver basic services to the population and found an ideal space to introduce themselves as a kind of power,[7] subjecting the *favela* communities to their political and economic interests, enforcing a kind of dictatorship, and developing rules, codes of conduct, and even tribunals held in the narrow alleyways of the *favelas*.[8]

## Drug trafficking and violence in the favelas

The drug traffic in Rio de Janeiro went through significant changes after the end of the 1970s with the arrival of cocaine. In the 1980s, the establishment and organization of drug factions took place. The entrance of cocaine into the retail drug market and its profitability were fundamental to the establishment and structure of these armed groups and the high levels of violence associated with them from the mid-1980s.[9] These transformations are related to the skyrocketing increase in the profitability generated by the drug market due to the high price of cocaine, the appearance of new factions, disputes over territories, and, as a consequence, a boost in the levels of violence.

With the emergence of the drug factions, a military structure was instituted either for defense or for invasions, and a division of labor was settled on for the preparation and sale of drugs. From the 1990s, with the establishment of two other drug factions, Third Command and ADA, an increase in territorial disputes, militarization, and violence occurred. At the same time, children and youth were recruited to trafficking, and armed conflicts began.[10]

Notwithstanding the fact that the great majority of those who live in the *favelas* are honest citizens who struggle to find legal work, in a country with high unemployment rates, slum inhabitants are subjected to the laws imposed by the traffickers. This "system of laws" was developed as a result of the immense gap left by an absent state, which took more than half a century to recognize and accept the *favela*s as an integral part of the city.

Dowdney calls attention to the process of behavioral changes within the *favela* communities before the 1980s and after the explosion of the drug business in the past two decades.[11] Some respect persists between factions and community residents and is fundamental to the coexistence of the slum inhabitants and drug traffickers. In the 1970s, the traffickers were more respectful toward the *favela* residents and family values, and they knew people in the community whom they had grown up with. During the late 1980s and 1990s, the murder of important leaders of the Comando Vermelho and the internal fragmentation of the organization facilitated the growth of rival factions and the fight for territory. With an increase of invasions in attempts to dominate *bocas de fumo* (the sales point for illicit drugs within a favela community) of rival factions, the number of traffickers from outside the community grew considerably. Because of the lack of a previous relationship between the traffickers and the community residents, the traffickers disregarded several of the considerations deemed to have value in older times. In addition, the state continued to neglect the needs of people living in these slums.

---

## Social integration in a disintegrated world: The lack of alternatives

Anhut and Heitmeyer assert in their theory of disintegration that "disintegration marks the failure of social institutions and communities to deliver existential basics, social recognition and personal integrity." Thus, a state that fails in its duty to deliver basic services, education, and health care, which would eventually lead to the social integration necessary to individuals coming from lower classes, mainly to youth, in their development as subjects with rights, has great responsibility for the level of crime and violence that characterizes cities like Rio de Janeiro today.[12]

Because of the lack of state presence, the social integration of slum dwellers with the rest of the city is weak and based generally on a demand for cheap labor from the asphalt. In fact, except for relationships based on labor needs of rich families that hire poor people to carry out low-level jobs, wealthy people avoid contact with the poor. The lack of social integration and the invisibility of the *favela* population entail several other problems, such as the need for social recognition and the search for ways to belong to this excluding society, even if it is through violence. As Anhut and Heitmeyer stressed, ". . . Every human being has a fundamental need to maintain and/or enhance self-esteem and that when it is diminished deviant acts are an appropriate, logical option for finding new recognition. . . . As regards social control motives, a lack of cooperative resources (absence of social skills, lack of education, status or prestige, etc.) is blamed for violent acts or the subjective existence of a belief that the individual's goals can only be achieved through violence. An absence of alternatives is the dominant pattern."[13] Certainly, deviant acts, power obtained through participating in criminal activities, and involvement with gangs that fulfill several of these needs are a logical option for young people for finding recognition and a sense of belonging.

Heitmeyer[14] relates joining a gang to a state of collective frustration among youths from lower social strata who are unable to achieve middle-class–oriented goals because of their lack of schooling and job skills. The lack of alternatives, whether in relation to schooling or a job, ends up pushing youth to join drug factions. The realization that they will have opportunities to compete successfully with others is another key point in determining the path that disadvantaged youth will follow.

## *The role of the police: A divided structure*

In addition to the violence inflicted by the criminals inside and outside the *favelas*, slum inhabitants are also constant victims of actions carried out by corrupt members of the Brazilian police force. Some of these police agents are known worldwide for their arbitrariness, abuse, close relationships with criminal organizations, and violence. Corruption is part of this as well. But other members of the police fight police corruption and try to establish relationships with slum inhabitants.

The Federative Republic of Brazil is composed of twenty-six states and a federal district, its capital. Brazil has a federal police department at the national level and a military and civil police at the state level.[15] The Brazilian constitution assigns most of the responsibility for criminal activity to state police forces, which are divided into two nearly autonomous entities: the civilian and military police. They are the forces responsible for day-to-day policing and are under the control of the states governors. The military police patrol the streets, maintain public order, and may arrest suspects caught in the act of committing a crime or pursuant to an arrest warrant issued by a judge. According to a government study carried out in 2002, the majority of the thirty-seven thousand military police in Rio are poorly educated young, black males.[16] The military police earn a salary of approximately US$410 per month, and they commonly hold a second job to augment this low salary.

The civil police are authorized to perform investigations, exercise the functions of criminal police, and investigate criminal offenses (investigative policing). They are responsible for dealing with most criminal activity, with the exception of the military. The military police are constitutionally responsible for public policing; arrests of those committing crimes are usually carried out by the military police, although the civil police sometimes act on such occasions.[17] Arresting officers are required to bring the suspect directly to a police precinct for processing. Police precincts are run by the civil police and headed by a precinct chief, who is required to hold a law degree. At this point, the military police have no further participation in the criminal investigation. Thus, the military police respond to crimes while they are in progress, and the civil police respond to crimes once they have occurred.

The lack of adequate training, proper equipment, and, most of all, an adequate salary opens the door to corruption and the involvement of police agents with criminal organizations. The low salaries of police in Rio de Janeiro, added to the lack of security when combating crime, of course do not justify the illegal and criminal actions that police engage in. Nevertheless, it shows how deeply rooted the problem is. Drug factions pay bribes to sustain a peaceful interaction and cordial relationship with some police.

It is worth mentioning, as Amnesty International acknowledged, that "the high rates of collusion with drug gangs, either to supplement meagre wages or as a means of self-protection, has seen police increasingly involved in criminal activity."[18] Dowdney also described police corruption and association with criminals: "The involvement of police officers in supplying illicit drugs and arms to drug gangs is also rife. . . . The relation between the police force and drug trafficking in Rio de Janeiro has shown itself to be intimately corrupted. . . . In almost all cases of the apprehension of drugs or contraband arms there exists the involvement of members of these corporations [the police]."[19]

The special rapporteur on extrajudicial, summary, or arbitrary executions, Asma Jahangir, on her mission to Brazil in October 2003, concluded that "the unanimous view was that all branches of the police—federal, military and civil—were corrupt. Each one is accused of excesses and is reported to have carried out extrajudicial and summary executions. At the same time it was the collective opinion—backed by ample information—that the military police had by far the worst record in violating human rights and perpetrating extrajudicial and summary executions."[20]

Because drug trafficking is economically oriented, the presence of the police in the *favelas*, either committing violent acts or attempting to repress the drug trade business, means the temporary suspension of business and consequently fewer sales and lower profits. Therefore, drug traffickers, profiting from the corruption inside both police forces, military and civil, use the language of money to keep their businesses running smoothly.

The irony behind these actions executed by the police, military or civil, is that we are in fact referring to the very individuals paid, trained, and equipped by the state, with funds provided by taxes and contributions paid by society as a whole, to protect the same society from crime and violence. What takes place in a city of contrasts like Rio de Janeiro is a violent and discriminatory public policing policy added to unlawful and illegal acts executed by the police,[21] substantially against the poorest communities whose poverty is associated with criminality. Added to this harsh reality is the violence inflicted by drug gangs inside the *favelas* against the residents and against those who disobey the orders or rules of conduct that these traffickers imposed.

The truth is that with the marginalization of a whole class, civil society feels relieved when another "criminal" (black, poor, and undereducated) is shot or arrested in another police incursion in the *favelas*. This is the way society expurgates its collective guilt. Taking into consideration the violations of basic human rights inflicted by the widespread violence, whether structural or armed, it is not so troublesome to imagine why some *favela* residents prefer to be bound by the laws of the drug traffickers rather than by the laws of the state.

## *How to break the pattern and bring the police closer to Rio society*

Nevertheless, recent initiatives of community policing and police reform show some light at the end of the tunnel. Among others, there is one experience from the military police that had the support of a civil society organization, Viva Rio, which is worth analyzing. The initiative was designed jointly by Viva Rio and the public security secretary of the State of Rio de Janeiro and was launched in July 2000. A new division was created within the Rio Military Police, called GPAE (Grupamento de Policiamento em Áreas Especiais), which roughly means "grouping for the policing of special areas."

The site chosen for the first experiment of the new division created within GPAE was Cantagalo and Pavão-Pavãozinho, a complex of *favelas* located in the heart of "marvelous Rio": the juncture of Copacabana, Ipanema, and Lagoa. Besides the consideration for the visibility and the beauty of the place, the choice came in

NEW DIRECTIONS FOR YOUTH DEVELOPMENT • DOI: 10.1002/yd

response to a serious riot in May 2000 with the burning of buses and breaking of windows by enraged *favela* dwellers after the alleged execution of five teenagers by members of the local police. The fact that it was a medium-size community, fairly isolated within a middle-class environment, also counted for its choice.

GPAE reports directly to the Central Command. It can thus focus on its single task: patrol of a well-defined and fairly isolated violent community within the city. One hundred men were recruited for the first experiment in Cantagalo and Pavão-Pavãozinho, a complex of about fifteen thousand inhabitants. This gives a ratio of one officer per 150 inhabitants, three times higher than the usual rate for the state of Rio. The police thus outnumbered the dealer's soldiers in this *favela*.

GPAE proposed and widely publicized the rules for its action in the community:

- Prohibition of the use of arms in the community
- Prohibition of children's involvement in drug dealing
- Prohibition of police violence and police corruption

The message was clear: the priority for GPAE was to cut violence down. The focus was small arms and their use by dealers and by police. Drug trafficking, a crime under Brazilian law, would not be condoned. GPAE's main concern, however, was the other end of the problem: the armed territorial control by parallel forces and its violent practices. The reference to children ("no children in drug dealing") led to another key element in the design of GPAE: the police should be associated with the social values recognized and approved by the community.

Recruited in July from among the regular ranks, the GPAE officers were trained over three months in a community-friendly approach. The mission and the training represented a radical innovation in relation to existing practices and perceptions. It is no wonder that they met with strong resistance from the recruits. The idea of patrolling on a regular basis, day and night, a labyrinth of dark, narrow, and dirty alleys, and constantly exposed to enemy fire,

seemed to them a senseless proposition. Thus, besides the indoc-
trination, the first training had mainly the impact of letting the
recruits know that the rules were to be applied. Used to discipline,
they would better adjust to the mission. The GPAE commander in
chief held a critical position. He had to believe in the mission and
make sure that the others would follow, whether they believed in
it or not. The following year, other training courses were introduced, with more interaction and understanding. Once GPAE was
functioning and became known in the *favelas*, the new recruits
could be engaged through voluntary request.

GPAE was not supposed to work alone. The other special unit
within the Rio Police had an opposite and yet complementary
nature: BOPE, "the men in black," was expert in high-risk situations
and armed confrontations. GPAE and BOPE would balance each
other, one acting as the "good cop" and the other as the "bad cop."

The start of this new initiative was crucial. In July 2000, the GPAE
commander started to visit the school, churches, associations, and
samba centers of the community to announce the new police program. A pamphlet was published in a news tabloid format, explaining the idea. Thousands of these pamphlets were distributed by police
at the entrances to the community at rush hour, when people were
going to and coming from work. The community as a whole and the
local powers in particular should not be taken by surprise by GPAE.

BOPE was the first to enter, a couple of months later, in September 2000. It did so openly, moving after repeated announcements,
at daylight and in great numbers, and heavily armed. It moved in
such a fashion in order to inhibit armed resistance. GPAE should
not begin by provoking a shoot-out. In the past when drug dealers
became aware that BOPE was coming, they hid and waited because
they knew that BOPE eventually would leave. This time, however,
BOPE stayed longer, and it left behind a new force: GPAE.

Between July and September, the GPAE commander met with
community leaders to discuss their social claims, such as better provision of public services, infrastructure, and activities for children
and youth, among others. A workshop was organized with the sup-

port of a businessman expert in group dynamics and strategic planning. Ministers, priests, cultural and sports coordinators, the presidents of two neighborhood associations, and others were invited to engage in positive planning for the future. Issues of water supply and of urbanization were first on the list and got a fast response. Programs for children and youth were equally emphasized and became the object of various actions by government and nongovernmental agencies.

Thus, the creation of GPAE was associated with two precious goods: an end to violence and the opening of social opportunities. Furthermore, to support these ideas and give them practical content, a community council was created, with the voluntary participation of every group in the community, to meet monthly with GPAE, identify problems, and propose solutions.

The impact of this project has been remarkable. In the first two years, homicides were reduced to zero and the shoot-outs ended. The armed gangs hid their guns and moved to more isolated areas of the hill. Instead of confronting the police at such close range daily, they chose to adjust their methods discretely to continue selling drugs in the tourist areas of Copacabana and Ipanema. GPAE kept its word concerning police behavior. Seventy officers of the initial one hundred were punished for misconduct and removed from the program. This consistent punishment of police misconduct, with formal recognition to the community council (something unheard of in the past), made the difference for the program's credibility. Furthermore, several NGOs promoted a range of projects, among which was Child Hope Space, a major initiative of sports, arts, and education for children and teenagers, coordinated by Viva Rio under the sponsorship of TV Globo and first UNICEF, and now UNESCO.

Other GPAEs were implemented in different communities; some were successful and others not. Changes in government led to a gradual erosion of GPAE's distinctive nature. To survive, it must grow, take root in other neighborhoods, and form its own tradition within the force and become a stronger reality, less vulnerable to leadership changes.

## Conclusion

Brazil is a democratic state. However, a democracy cannot be fully implemented when the great majority of the population, especially young, poor Brazilians, have no access to fundamental rights and are systematically excluded from the path toward a dignified life. Soares, Bill, and Athayde assert in *Cabeça de Porco* that "the crime in Brazil is a defeat of all of us, a shared failure."[22] In fact, marginalization and oppression of a specific class existed in Brazil before 1964, during the dictatorship, and continues to exist under the flag of the democratic government today. Children and youth, victims of prejudice and indifference, wander in the streets of Rio, receiving constantly scared and reproving looks from the citizens of the asphalt. Several of them were expelled from the *favelas* by the drug gangs that were managing the drug trade business, losing their contact with family members and their last referential. Poor Brazilians still face police brutality, discrimination, and a series of injustices and arbitrariness in their daily life.

Regarding the police and its actions as a state agent, it is worth addressing the role they play in Rio's drug trade. The main objective of the police forces is to protect citizens' rights and constitutional freedoms and enforce the law. But if, in enforcing the law, force is used, police will regard it as legitimate to use. When police enter the slums in order to "enforce the law," many times what is seen are mothers panicking and running through the narrow alleyways of the *favelas* in order to take their children out of harm's way. Some police agents do not differ from dangerous traffickers and the great majority of slum residents. Nevertheless, the relationship between the drug traffickers and the *favela* communities is moving through a transformation, due mainly to two factors. One is the increase in indiscriminate violence by the drug traffickers inside the *favelas*. The extreme level of violence employed by the traffickers causes a countereffect among the *favela* communities.

If the state's social institutions were looking for the right time to attempt to work in the *favelas* and to build a closer relationship with the *favela* communities, now seems to be a favorable time. *Favela* residents are beginning to change their behavior toward traffickers for a number of reasons. First, the cruelty and brutality of drug traffickers have reached an almost unbearable level, frightening *favela* residents who no longer can count on any respect and protection.[23] Second, the widespread violence routinely employed by the traffickers against anyone who dares to defy their supremacy and orders is generating growing discontent among the *favelados*. Finally, the young poor are joining drug gangs because of a lack of other options and to belong to a structure that accepts them and provides them some power.

The other factor relates to successful experiences such as GPAE at Cantagalo. However, GPAE is just as vulnerable to corruption by the local dealers as the police in general are. Some argue that given the inevitable coexistence, it may become even more exposed to corruption than other units. This is a debatable criticism, since daily violence forms the best environment for daily corruption (one negotiates life). Nonetheless, GPAE has been stung by reports of corruption and loss of control, and it still has to develop a consistent anticorruption program. Corruption brings the guns back. The fight against corruption needs a combination of internal and external controls. The external control, which is the more effective, depends on community trust, which itself depends on how effective GPAE is. Hence, it seems that good management of this experience is key to ensuring that it will endure.

To improve on the experience and open a new chapter in police practices in Brazil, GPAE needs something more: a proactive style of policing. Current behavior, common to police in Brazil in general, is basically reactive: officers wait for something to happen.

An active approach is needed instead, where officers go to the streets with a specific agenda to help solve problems that lead to disorder and violence, fulfilling the preventive mission of their presence. Given an agenda, daily action may be planned, evaluated, and improved.

Above all, it should not be forgotten that only a minority of *favela* residents are involved in the drug trade. Nevertheless, all *favela* residents suffer from daily violence, structural or armed.

The young people who become involved in criminal activities probably entered this path pushed by all the circumstances discussed in this article and also impelled by the deep feeling of revolt generated by overwhelming social inequalities, discrimination, and a lack of other opportunities.[24]

## Notes

1. Information obtained from the Brazilian Institute of Geography and Statistics (IBGE), census of 2005.

2. Asphalt or (*asfalto*) refers to the areas of the city that are not considered to be in the *favela*.

3. Flat slums are also part of Rio de Janeiro's scenario; like the *favela* City of God (Cidade de Deus), most *favelas* are located on the hillsides.

4. Zaluar, A., & Alvito, M. (2003). *Um Século de Favelas*. Rio de Janeiro: FGV.

5. Barcellos, C. (2004). *Abusado—O Dono do Morro Dona Marta*. São Paulo: Record. p. 64.

6. Reurbanization refers to the implementation of basic urban services that still do not exist in many slums, such as sanitation services, solid waste management, waste collection, cleaning of drains, transforming narrow alleyways into paved streets, and so on.

7. Dowdney, L. (2003). *Children of the drug trade: A case study of children in organised armed violence in Rio de Janeiro, Viva Rio/ISER*. Rio de Janeiro: 7 Letras. p. 70. Dowdney presents a theory that drug factions cannot be seen as a parallel state or power but should be seen as a "concurrent presence" regarding sociopolitical control of *favela* populations. He argues that factions' control of the community is the result of the government's inability to be completely present in the *favela* and that it is due to the almost total abandonment by state government of *favela* communities over the last fifty years that faction domination and control of *favelas* was made possible. Drug faction control of *favela* populations has not come about due to their ability to supersede the state from a political, social, or military perspective. They have simply filled a space that the government has failed to occupy."

8. Huguet, C. (2005). *The dictatorship of the drug traffic in the slums of Rio de Janeiro vs the international and national human rights law*. Unpublished L.L.M dissertation, University of Utrecht.

9. Amorim, C. (2004). *CV_PCC A Irmandade do Crime*. São Paulo: Record.

10. Dowdney, L. (2003). *Children of the drug trade: A case study of children in organised armed violence in Rio de Janeiro, Viva Rio/ISER*. Rio de Janeiro: 7 Letras. p. 73.

11. Dowdney. (2003).

12. Anhut, R., & Heitmeyer, W. (2006). Disintegration, recognition and violence. *Les Cahiers de Psychologie politique*, no. 9, 1.

13. Anhut, R., & Heitmeyer, W. (2006). Disintegration, recognition and violence. *Les Cahiers de Psychologie politique*, p. 5.

14. Anhut, R., & Heitmeyer, W. (2006). Disintegration, recognition and violence. *Les Cahiers de Psychologie politique*, p. 4.

15. The federal police, who are relatively small, cover federal crimes such as terrorism, organized crime, federal fiscal crimes, border and immigration control, and responsibility over indigenous peoples.

16. Núcleo de Pesquisa e Análise Criminal, State Secretariat for Public Security. Study available at www.nova policia.rj.gov.br.

17. Article 301 of the Criminal Procedure Code provides that "any citizen may and the police authority and its agents shall arrest anyone caught in the act of committing a crime."

18. Amnesty International. (2003). *Candelária e Vigário Geral 10 years on*/AI Index: AMR 19/015/2003, Brazil, 8. http://web.amnesty.org/library/Index/ENGAMR190172003?open&of=ENG-BRA.

19. Werneck and Rocha 1999 as referenced in Dowdney. (2003). P. 89.

20. Report of the Special Rapporteur, Asma Jahangir—Civil and Political Rights, including the question of disappearances and summary executions, visit carried out from September 16 to October 8, 2003—E/CN.4/2004/7/Add.3, January 28th 2004, 85.

21. Cano, I. (1997). *Letalidade da Ação Policial no Rio de Janeiro*. Rio de Janeiro: ISER.

22. Soares, L. E., Bill, M., & Athayde, C. (2005). *Cabeça de Porco*. Rio de Janeiro: Objetiva. P. 90.

23. Barcellos. (2004). P. 217.

24. Soares et al. (2005). p. 125. The authors stress that the most difficult task is the one to humanize the criminal without taking responsibility for his actions and, most important, recognizing the responsibility of the system existent in Brazil as a whole.

CLARISSA HUGUET *is the coordinator of the COAV Cities Project at the Brazilian NGO Viva-Rio.*

ILONA SZABÓ DE CARVALHO *is the senior program coordinator of Synergos Institute in Brazil. She was the coordinator of the Human Security Program at the Brazilian NGO Viva Rio from November 2005 to July 2008.*

*The origins of youth violence can be traced in part to the experience of recognition denial and a resulting need for autonomy.*

# 7

# Recognition denial, need for autonomy, and youth violence

*Timothy Brezina*

OVER THE PAST FEW DECADES, the autonomy needs of adolescents have received growing attention from criminologists. Indeed, a number of contemporary theorists identify youths' need (or desire) for autonomy as a fundamental motivation for criminal and delinquent involvement.[1] For example, some theorists believe that delinquent behavior is attractive to young people because it provides an expedient way to realize a limited sense of freedom or independence in the face of adult rules and restrictions. According to Moffitt, "Every curfew violated, car stolen, drug taken, and baby conceived is a statement of personal independence and thus a reinforcer for delinquent involvement."[2]

Although data in this area are limited, previous studies provide empirical support for the idea that delinquency may stem in part from adolescents' demands for autonomy and independence. Drawing on data from a large sample of male adolescents in the United States, Agnew finds that many young men report a strong need for autonomy, expressed by a chief desire "to be free from the control of others."[3] Although the strength of this need varies considerably from individual to individual, adolescents who report a

NEW DIRECTIONS FOR YOUTH DEVELOPMENT, NO. 119, FALL 2008 © WILEY PERIODICALS, INC.
Published online in Wiley InterScience (www.interscience.wiley.com) • DOI: 10.1002/yd.276

very strong need for autonomy tend to exhibit relatively high levels of delinquent behavior, including interpersonal violence.

Based on field observations, Jacobs concludes that a strong need for autonomy serves to diminish the perceived attractiveness of legitimate work, which typically restricts movement and involves taking orders from others.[4] This fact may help to explain why some young people are drawn to the illicit (and often violent) drug trade and to other sources of illegitimate income.[5] As Jacobs describes, "The cultural ethos of the streetcorner renders any form of subordination unacceptable. This ethos is part of a larger resentment of authority, external control, and restrictions on behavior that many street offenders feel deeply."[6]

Although a relationship between need for autonomy and youth offending has been documented in previous studies, the following question remains largely unexplored: Why do some young people develop an exaggerated need for autonomy in the first place? An answer to this question is important because greater knowledge of the origins of autonomy needs may improve our understanding of the underlying causes of youth crime and violence.

The purpose of the study examined here is to take an initial step in this direction. Drawing on relevant theoretical work, especially the recognition or integration theory of violence as elaborated by Anhut and Heitmeyer,[7] I seek to explain why some adolescents develop an exaggerated need for autonomy and, hence, why they are prone to acts of crime and violence. Also, although previous studies have linked autonomy needs to a wide range of minor and serious delinquent acts,[8] I explore the contribution of such needs to interpersonal violence in particular.

I hypothesize that a strong need for autonomy (or "me-first" attitude) tends to develop partly in reaction to social interactions with adults that young people experience as frustrating, humiliating, unfair, or threatening to their worth and dignity. It is expected that such interactions will tend to diminish young people's interest in social cooperation and will foster the expression of exaggerated self-assertion. The development of a strong need for autonomy is one possible consequence of exaggerated self-assertion, and for a number of reasons, this need tends to increase the likelihood of violent behavior. Data from a large survey of male adolescents are used to assess the plausibility of the hypothesized relationships.

## Explaining individual variation in the need for autonomy

*Autonomy* has been defined as "power over oneself, the ability to resist the demands of others, and to engage in action without the permission of others."[9] According to developmental psychologists, an important challenge of adolescence is to develop autonomy of this sort without simultaneously damaging parental relationships.[10] Most young people meet this challenge successfully. Adolescents typically seek to gain more control over their lives and the family decisions that affect them, "but not at the expense of maintaining strong, positive relationships with their parents."[11] In short, most adolescents are interested in striking a healthy balance between their desire for autonomy and their desire to maintain family relatedness.

Why, then, do some adolescents demand their autonomy above all else, at the expense of family or community relations? Recognition or integration theory, as elaborated by Anhut and Heitmeyer, appears to be especially relevant to this issue.[12] According to recognition theory, the balancing of personal freedom and social attachment helps to promote the successful integration of the individual into community life. Under conditions of successful social integration, the provision of recognition is possible, and the socioemotional needs of the individual can be met (for example, emotional warmth or support, a sense of belonging, a sense that one is important or valued). When such needs are met, the voluntary acceptance of norms and constraints is typically achieved.

Conversely, in the event of unsuccessful integration, and as a result of an accompanying lack or denial of recognition, the acceptance of norms and constraints becomes problematic. The lack or denial of recognition can take many forms, including the denial of

positional recognition (experienced as a perceived lack of importance, worth, or significance to the community), denial of moral recognition (unfair or unequal treatment), and denial of emotional
recognition (lack of emotional support, esteem, or attention). Denial
of positional, moral, or emotional recognition tends to generate negative emotional and behavioral consequences at the level of the individual, such as apathy or resignation; feelings of weakness or
inferiority; the experience of humiliation, rage, or a sense of injustice; or lack of empathy or concern for others.[13] Some of these consequences may serve to lower thresholds for violent behavior and in
general contribute to the development of antisocial conduct.

Some antisocial behaviors appear to represent fairly direct
responses to problems of recognition, as in the case of individuals
who use violence to compensate for feelings of personal weakness
or inferiority.[14] However, problems of recognition may contribute
to antisocial behavior indirectly by fostering attitudes that are anti-
thetical to social cooperation. For instance, treatment by others
that is perceived to be unfair or manipulative may lead to the development of a "general dislike and suspicion of others and an associated tendency to respond in an aggressive manner."[15] Such attitudes
and biases are also highlighted by the social information model of
aggression.[16]

Problems associated with recognition denial may lead to the
development of attitudes that promote egocentric pursuits, generate hostility toward authority, and—indirectly—increase the likelihood of antisocial behavior. For example, individuals who
experience a persistent recognition deficit and therefore reap few
meaningful rewards from community life probably have little
incentive to restrain their egoistic desires for the benefit of the
community. Moreover, if participation in community life fails to
provide recognition, and if it offers nothing in return for confor-
mity, then individuals would have less reason to tolerate the many
rules and restrictions inherent in community life. As Durkheim
observed, "The more weakened the groups to which [the individ-
ual] belongs, the less he depends on them, the more he conse-

quently depends only on himself and recognizes no other rules of conduct than what are founded on his private interests."[17]

Reduced tolerance for societal constraints, along with the accompanying development of a me-first attitude, may well be responsible for the strong need for autonomy expressed by some young people in earlier studies.[18] Indeed, a strong need for autonomy may reflect a specific and particularly criminogenic form of the me-first attitude that has been of concern to recognition and integration theorists.[19] According to Agnew, young people who express a strong need for autonomy say they "demand freedom and independence above everything else" and "argue against people who try to boss" them around.[20]

A strong need for autonomy may also reflect a form of defensive independence. Having been denied recognition by others (in reality or perception), individuals may have a tendency to respond defensively in an effort to protect their sense of self. For example, they may respond by saying, "To hell with you! I don't need anybody else anyway. I will be my own boss and will follow my own rules."[21]

Adolescents may be especially likely to develop such attitudes in response to problems of recognition. In contrast to most adults, adolescents lack social power and thus are compelled to live with their family in a particular neighborhood, go to a certain school, and generally interact with the same groups of people over time. Moreover, society gives parents and teachers "considerable legitimate advantages in controlling adolescents," and deference is expected in most interactions with adults, even as society encourages the adolescent to strive for independence.[22] When experienced in the context of relationships that are demeaning, humiliating, and threatening to the adolescent's sense of self, these limitations on freedom and independence are likely to be especially painful or frustrating, and the importance of personal autonomy is likely to be felt as never before.

It should be noted that limitations on freedom and independence do not by themselves necessarily lead to an exaggerated need or desire for autonomy.[23] So long as relationships with parents and

teachers are valued by the adolescent for the recognition they provide, the general acceptance of constraints is not likely to be problematic. What is crucial to the development of an exaggerated need
for autonomy, then, is not simply a lack of real autonomy, but
rather the experience of limited autonomy in the context of painful
or frustrating relationships characterized by recognition denial.

## The criminogenic consequences of a strong need for autonomy

A strong or exaggerated need for autonomy is likely to be criminogenic for at least three reasons. First, criminal and delinquent
behaviors may be attractive to individuals who have a strong need
for autonomy because these behaviors may symbolize freedom and
independence.[24] In the eyes of the frustrated adolescent, for
instance, delinquency may symbolize an ability to defy the rules and
restrictions of those in control.[25] Thus, delinquent conduct, including physical aggression, may serve to affirm the adolescent's personal independence in the face of adult constraints and impositions.

Second, criminal and delinquent acts may allow frustrated adolescents to achieve objective control or autonomy.[26] For instance,
young people may be able to exercise immediate control and
greater autonomy through the use of force or threat of force. Like-
wise, a reputation for being violent or aggressive may intimidate
others—including peers, parents, and teachers—and cause them to
avoid confrontation or rule enforcement.[27] Such behaviors, then,
may be especially appealing to youths who possess a strong need
for autonomy.

Third, a strong need for autonomy may contribute to attitudes
and emotions that are generally conducive to antisocial behavior,
such as lack of concern for the well-being of others, resentment of
authority, and disdain for the controls that normally serve to inhibit
violence or physical harm. As Agnew confirmed, youths who possess a strong need for autonomy tend to have weak social bonds and
are prone to anger and frustration, and these facts help to account

for the effect of autonomy needs on delinquency, including interpersonal violence.[28]

## Hypotheses

In sum, recognition theory appears to provide a useful theoretical
framework for understanding the development of me-first attitudes
among young people, including a strong need for autonomy. This
need appears to be implicated in the development of antisocial
behaviors, including youth violence, as suggested by the existing
research literature on crime and delinquency. Specifically, it is possible to derive the following testable hypotheses from the above
discussion:

HYPOTHESIS 1. *Perceived recognition denial is positively associated with
the development of a strong need for autonomy.*
HYPOTHESIS 2. *A strong need for autonomy is associated with the development of violent behavior (interpersonal aggression).*

The first hypothesis is novel to this study. A test of this hypothesis is the main focus of the data analyses described here, as the
results may have implications for the plausibility of the recognition
theory of violence. A test of the second hypothesis provides an
opportunity to replicate the findings of prior criminological
research using, in this case, statistical procedures that are relatively
advanced. Taken together, these two hypotheses will be used to
guide an examination of the dynamic interrelationships between
perceived recognition denial, autonomy needs, and youth violence.

## Data and methods

To assess the plausibility of the hypothesized relationships
described, data were drawn from the Youth in Transition (YIT) survey, a multiwave panel survey based on a nationwide sample of male

public high school students in the United States. This is the same data set Agnew used to examine the relationship between the need for autonomy and delinquency.[29] To my knowledge, it is the only panel survey of its kind containing a need-for-autonomy scale. The YIT data have been used in a number of delinquency studies[30] and are available to member universities through the Inter-University Consortium of Political and Social Research.

The initial wave of data collection took place in fall 1966. Personal interview and questionnaire data were obtained from 2,213 male youths as they were entering their sophomore year. The boys were selected through the use of multistage probability sampling, and according to the authors of the study, the resulting sample constituted "an essentially bias-free representation of tenth-grade boys in public high schools throughout the United States."[31] The second wave of data was collected from 1,886 respondents (85 percent of the time 1 sample) in the spring of their junior year (approximately a year and a half later).

Data presented by Bachman, O'Malley, and Johnston indicate that the survey results were not seriously biased by either panel attrition or repeated measurement effects. In particular, respondents lost to attrition were slightly more likely than regular participants to live in urban areas, come from broken homes, be black, and be of lower socioeconomic status. In most cases the difference was small, "usually less than five percent of a standard deviation."[32]

*Measures*

To construct various measures for this study, items similar in content were factor-analyzed, and items that loaded onto a single factor were selected to form various scales. The scale items are equally weighted, and the average of these items constitutes the scale score. Table 7.1 presents descriptive statistics for the major variables in the study (see the article appendix for a complete description of the major theoretical constructs).

The research strategy for this study involves an examination of current (time 2) variables, while controlling for prior levels of certain other (time 1) variables, including prior levels of perceived recogni-

Table 7.1.  **Descriptive statistics for the major variables**

| Variable | Mean | SD | Range |
|---|---|---|---|
| Interpersonal Aggression (time 1) | 1.54 | .58 | 1.00–5.00 |
| Interpersonal Aggression (time 2) | 1.24 | .45 | 1.00–5.00 |
| Need for Autonomy (time 1) | 3.53 | .71 | 1.40–5.00 |
| Need for Autonomy (time 2) | 3.37 | .72 | 1.20–5.00 |
| Perceived Rejection (time 1) | 2.37 | .80 | 1.00–5.00 |
| Perceived Rejection (time 2) | 2.34 | .78 | 1.00–5.00 |
| Parental Punitiveness (time 1) | 2.48 | .78 | 1.00–5.00 |
| Parental Punitiveness (time 2) | 2.39 | .72 | 1.00–5.00 |
| Mean Teacher (time 1) | 2.89 | .67 | 1.00–5.00 |
| Mean Teacher (time 2) | 2.69 | .61 | 1.00–5.00 |
| Perceived Recognition Denial (time 1) | 2.55 | .53 | 1.00–5.00 |
| Perceived Recognition Denial (time 2) | 2.46 | .51 | 1.00–5.00 |
| Family Structure (1 = lives with both parents) | .79 | .41 | 0–1 |
| Race (1 = nonwhite) | .13 | .34 | 0–1 |
| Socioeconomic status (SES) | 5.02 | .80 | 2.62–7.27 |

tion denial, need for autonomy, and violent behavior. Thus, most of the items described below were measured at both points in time.

*Perceived Recognition Denial.*  Several scales index perceived lack or denial of recognition, especially the denial of emotional recognition and, to a lesser extent, the denial of moral and positional recognition (for example, blamed unfairly, treated as an inferior, viewed as unworthy). Respondents who obtain high scores on a three-item measure called Perceived Rejection say they often feel that "nobody wants me," often feel "lonesome," and rarely "feel loved" (Cronbach's alpha reliability score at time 2 = .67). High scorers on a five-item Parental Punitiveness scale say their parents often slap, threaten to slap, yell, nag, and give out undeserved blame (alpha = .76). High scorers on a three-item Mean Teachers scale say their teachers mainly provide negative comments about their schoolwork, often lose their tempers, and frequently "talk down" to students and act as if students do not know anything (alpha = .55).

To facilitate the data analysis, a summary measure of perceived recognition denial was constructed by taking the average of the Perceived Rejection, Parental Punitiveness, and Mean Teacher scales. This summary scale should help to capture joint variation in the various types of recognition denial.

*Need for Autonomy.* Following Agnew, a five-item Need for Autonomy scale was constructed.[33] Respondents who obtain high scores on this scale say they "demand freedom and independence above everything," like to be their "own boss," "become stubborn when others try to force them to do something," "argue against people who try to boss" them around, and value "freedom from the control of others" as a life goal (alpha = .72).

*Interpersonal Aggression.* The YIT survey already contained an eight-item scale measuring the extent of the respondent's self-reported involvement in various aggressive and violent acts, including serious fights with peers, gang fights, robbery, and hitting their mother, father, or teachers. Response categories for each item in the scale range from 1 (never committed the act) to 5 (committed the act five or more times). The average of these items constitutes the scale score. During the first wave of the YIT survey, the recall period for the interpersonal aggression scale was the previous three years. During the second wave, the recall period was the time since the first wave of data collection (approximately one and a half years).

*Control variables.* The data analysis includes controls for socio-economic status (SES), family stability, and race. Socioeconomic status is measured by a six-item index constructed by the original investigators,[34] which combines information on father's occupational status, father's education, mother's education, number of rooms per person in the home, number of books in the home, and a checklist of other possessions (for example, a map or globe, a set of encyclopedias). The mean of the six items constitutes the scale score. Family stability is indexed by a dummy variable (1 = respondent lives with both his mother and father). Race is also indexed by a dummy variable (1 = nonwhite).

### Research strategy

To explore the dynamic interrelationships between perceived recognition denial, need for autonomy, and youth violence, a structural equation model was estimated using the weighted-least-squares (WLS) procedure available in LISREL 8.[35] The basic model to be estimated is shown in Figure 7.1. This model assumes

**Figure 7.1. Path model linking recognition denial, need for autonomy, and youth violence**

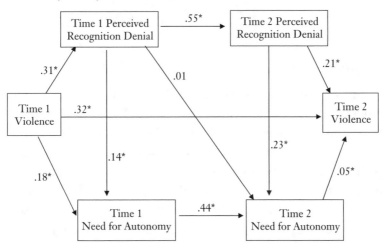

*Note:* Standardized WLS estimates are presented. Paths to all endogenous variables control for Family Stability, Race, and SES. To reduce visual clutter, the effects of these control variables are not shown.

$^*p < .05.$

that perceived recognition denial exerts both lagged and contemporaneous effects on need for autonomy. The model also assumes that the effect of perceived recognition denial on interpersonal aggression is mediated in part by the need for autonomy. In other words, it is proposed (consistent with the hypotheses) that perceived recognition denial contributes to a strong need for autonomy, which increases the likelihood of youth violence.

This model exploits the longitudinal nature of the data and includes controls for prior (time 1) levels of the main variables as well as controls for SES, Race, and Family Structure (to reduce visual clutter, the paths involving these control variables are not shown). The inclusion of prior need for autonomy, prior recognition denial, and prior violence effectively transforms the time 2 dependent variables into measures of change from one wave to the next. Thus, the significant predictors in the equation can be interpreted as predictors of change in the dependent variables over time.

This research strategy helps to increase confidence in proper causal ordering.

## Results

Figure 7.1 also presents the results of the model estimation. This model provides an excellent fit to the data. The chi-square statistic, with five degrees of freedom, is 6.70 ($p$ = .24). The adjusted goodness-of-fit index is .99. As seen in Figure 7.1, the hypothesized paths are all statistically significant, except for the lagged effect between time 1 Perceived Recognition Denial and time 2 Need for Autonomy. It appears, then, that the effect of recognition denial is mainly contemporaneous in nature, although it should be noted that the failure to observe a lagged effect may be due to the substantial period of time that separates the waves of data collection (approximately one and a half years).

Overall, the results of the model estimation indicate that (1) perceived recognition denial exerts a significant contemporaneous effect on need for autonomy, even after controlling for prior need for autonomy, and (2) the need for autonomy exerts a significant contemporaneous effect on violence, even after controlling for prior violent behavior. Further examination of the results reveals that the indirect effect of time 2 Perceived Recognition Denial on violence is statistically significant ($p$ < .05). Thus, although the effect of "need for autonomy" on violence is relatively weak in the model (.05), this variable still mediates part of the effect of recognition denial on violent behavior.

In general, the pattern of results observed in Figure 7.1 is consistent with expectations derived from recognition theory and existing criminological research. Among male adolescents, perceived recognition denial appears to contribute to the development of a strong need for autonomy, which contributes to the development of violent behavior.

It should be noted that the direct effect of recognition denial on violence is stronger than the indirect effect that operates through need for autonomy. Evidently recognition denial contributes to youth violence for the reasons given above and beyond the development of a strong need for autonomy. This fact suggests that to maximize impact, prevention and rehabilitation efforts should target the experience of recognition denial rather than autonomy-related attitudes. Several possible interventions are discussed next.

## Conclusion

In this study, the possible roots of an exaggerated need for autonomy were explored, drawing on relevant work in adolescent development and criminological theory, especially the recognition theory of violence elaborated by Anhut and Heitmeyer.[36] These works suggest that the roots of a strong need for autonomy can be traced in part to a lack or denial of recognition, including lack of emotional warmth and support, unfair or unequal treatment, and the perception of being regarded as unworthy or insignificant by others.

Recognition denial may contribute to an exaggerated need for autonomy and other me-first attitudes for several reasons. First, recognition denial is likely to reduce the individual's tolerance for community rules and restrictions, and hence increase one's felt need for autonomy and independence. Second, individuals may tend to respond to recognition denial with defensive independence: "To hell with you! I don't need anybody else anyway. I will be my own boss and will follow my own rules."[37]

Longitudinal data from the YIT study provide initial empirical support for the hypothesized relationship between recognition denial and need for autonomy. Controlling for other relevant variables, these data indicate that the development of a strong need for autonomy among male adolescents is partly a function of perceived recognition denial. A strong need for autonomy in turn is associated with the development of violent behavior.

These findings are noteworthy for several reasons. First, the results suggest that the recognition theory of violence provides a useful framework for understanding the development of attitudes that are conducive to violent behavior. Second, the findings may have implications for the control and prevention of youth violence. In particular, they appear to provide additional justification for interventions that are designed to foster relationships of mutual respect between young people and adults. Examples of such interventions include parenting programs designed to promote authoritative parenting practices (such as a fair but firm nurturing approach) and teacher training programs that encourage the use of positive reinforcement.[38] To the extent that such interventions promote perceived recognition, they may reduce the development of me-first attitudes and related antisocial behavior.

Third, the findings encourage additional research on the role of autonomy needs in the production of antisocial behavior. Research in this area remains limited, despite the important role assigned to autonomy needs by a number of leading theorists.[39]

As a starting point, future research could address the limitations of this study. First, the data examined in this study are limited to male adolescents. Although males appear to place greater importance on personal autonomy[40] and are more likely to engage in violent behavior, additional studies should be conducted to determine whether the findings also apply to female youths. Some studies suggest that the experience of frustrated autonomy among female adolescents may contribute to parental conflict, problems at school, and possibly delinquent behavior.[41] The processes observed in this study, then, may not be limited to male adolescents.

Second, an examination of more recent data is desirable. The YIT data are several decades old, and it is possible that the processes related to adolescent autonomy have changed over time. The statements of contemporary theorists,[42] along with the findings of more recent qualitative studies,[43] suggest that autonomy needs continue to play a role in the etiology of youth crime and violence. In fact, some theorists argue that personal autonomy has become more important to young people over the years,[44] suggesting that the processes examined in this study may operate with greater force today. Nonetheless, these expectations should be verified with current data.

Further examination of these issues will likely require the collection of new data because few existing surveys include measures that index the respondents' desire or need for autonomy. The results of this initial examination, however, suggest that such efforts are likely to be fruitful.

## Appendix: Measures of major theoretical constructs

### Need for Autonomy

1. I demand freedom and independence above everything else.
2. I become stubborn when others try to force me to do something.
3. I like to be on my own and to be my own boss.
4. I argue against people who try to boss me around.
5. One of my goals in life is to be free of the control of others.

### Perceived Rejection

1. [How often do you feel that] nobody wants you?
2. Feel lonesome?
3. Feel loved? [coding for this item reversed]

### Parental Punitiveness

1. [How often do your parents] actually slap you?
2. Threaten to slap you?
3. Yell, shout, or scream at you?
4. Nag at you?
5. Blame you or criticize you when you don't deserve it?

### Mean Teacher

1. How often do teachers at this school "talk down" to students, and act as if students don't know anything?
2. Do most of your teachers give you positive suggestions about your school work, or just make negative criticisms?
3. How often at this school do teachers lose their tempers?

*Interpersonal Aggression*

Since the last survey, how many times have you:

1. Got into a serious fight with a student in school?
2. Taken part in a fight where a bunch of your friends are against another bunch?
3. Got something by telling a person something bad would happen to him if you did not get what you wanted?
4. Used a knife or gun or some other thing (like a club) to get something from a person?
5. Hurt someone badly enough to need bandages or a doctor?
6. Hit a teacher?
7. Hit your father?
8. Hit your mother?

### Notes

1. Agnew, R. (1984). Autonomy and delinquency. *Sociological Perspectives*, *27*, 219–240; Greenberg, D. F. (1977). Delinquency and the age structure of society. *Contemporary Crises*, *1*, 189–223; Jacobs, B. A. (1999). *Dealing crack: The social world of streetcorner selling*. Boston: Northeastern University Press; Jacobs, B. A., & Wright, R. (1999). Stick-up, street culture, and offender motivation. *Criminology*, *37*, 149–173; Moffitt, T. E. (1993). Adolescence-limited and life-course-persistent antisocial behavior: A developmental taxonomy. *Psychological Review*, *100*, 674–701; Tittle, C. R. (1995). *Control balance: Toward a general theory of deviance*. Boulder, CO: Westview Press.
2. Moffitt. (1993). pp. 688–689.
3. Agnew. (1984). p. 225.
4. Jacobs. (1999).
5. Also see Jacobs & Wright. (1999); Shover, N., & Honaker, D. (1992). The socially bounded decision making of persistent property offenders. *Howard Journal of Criminal Justice*, *31*(4), 276–293.
6. Jacobs. (1999). p. 32.
7. Anhut, R., & Heitmeyer, W. (2006). *Disintegration, recognition and violence*. http://a.dorna.free.fr/RevueNo9/Rubrique2/R2SR1.htm
8. Agnew. (1984).
9. Agnew. (1984). p. 220; Marwell, G. (1966). Adolescent powerlessness and delinquent behavior. *Social Forces*, *14*, 35–47.
10. Eccles, J. S., Buchanan, C. M., Flanagan, C., Fuligni, A., Midgley, C., & Yee, D. (1991). Control versus autonomy during early adolescence. *Journal of Social Issues*, *47*, 53–68; Kuperminc, G. P., Allen, J. P., & Arthur, M. W. (1996). Autonomy, relatedness, and male adolescent delinquency: Toward a

multidimensional view of social competence. *Journal of Adolescent Research, 11*, 397–420; Murphey, E. B., Silber, E., Coelho, G. V., Hamburg, D. A., & Greenberg, I. (1963). Development of autonomy and parent-child interaction in late adolescence. *American Journal of Orthopsychiatry, 33*, 643–52.

11. Eccles et al. (1991). p. 64.

12. Anhut & Heitmeyer. (2007).

13. Anhut & Heitmeyer. (2007).

14. Anhut & Heitmeyer. (2007).

15. Agnew. (1992). Foundation for a general strain theory of crime and delinquency. *Criminology, 30*, 47–87.

16. Crick, N. R., & Dodge, K. A. (1996). Social information-processing mechanisms in reactive and proactive aggression. *Child Development, 67*, 993–1002.

17. Durkheim, E. (1951). *Suicide: A study in sociology* (John A. Spaulding & George Simpson, Trans.). New York: Free Press. p. 209. (Original work published 1897)

18. Agnew. (1984); Jacobs. (1999).

19. Anhut & Heitmeyer. (2007).

20. Agnew. (1984)

21. Rohner, R. P., Khaleque, A., & Cournoyer, D. E. (2005). Parental acceptance-rejection theory, methods, evidence, and implications. *Ethos: Journal of the Society for Psychological Anthropology, 33*(3), 299–334.

22. Marwell. (1966). p. 40.

23. See Agnew. (1984).

24. Agnew. (1984); Moffitt. (1993).

25. Brezina, T. (2000). Delinquency, control maintenance, and the negation of fatalism. *Justice Quarterly, 17*, 779–803.

26. Agnew. (1984).

27. Anderson. (1999). *Code of the street: Decency, violence, and the moral life of the inner city.* New York: Norton; Brezina, T. (1999). Teenage violence toward parents as an adaptation to family strain: Evidence from a national survey of male adolescents. *Youth and Society, 30*, 416–444.

28. Agnew. (1984).

29. Agnew. (1984).

30. See Agnew. (1985). A revised strain theory of delinquency. *Social Forces, 64*, 151–167; Brezina. (1999); Felson, R. B., Liska, A. E., South, S. J., & McNulty, T. L. (1994). The subculture of violence and delinquency: Individual vs. school context effects. *Social Forces, 73*, 155–173.

31. Bachman, J. G. (1975). *Young men in high school and beyond documentation manual.* Ann Arbor, MI: Institute for Social Research. p. 1.

32. Bachman, J. G., O'Malley, P. M., & Johnston, J. (1978). *Youth in transition: Adolescence to adulthood.* Ann Arbor, MI: Institute for Social Research. Following previous longitudinal studies that have used these data, the analyses in the study reported here are based on unweighted data. Although Bachman and his colleagues conclude that the survey results were not seriously biased by panel attrition, it should be noted that the possibility of nonresponse bias remains. Although correction techniques for such bias have become popular in criminology, experts caution that such techniques do not provide a magic

solution, are overused and frequently misapplied, and require knowledge of the source and magnitude of the bias to be used properly. See Bushway, S., Johnson, B., & Slocum, L. A. (2007). Is the magic still there? The use of the Heckman two-step correction for selection bias in criminology. *Journal of Quantitative Criminology, 23,* 151–178.

33. Agnew. (1984).

34. Bachman. (1975).

35. Joreskog, K. G., & Sorbom, D. (1993). *LISREL 8.* Hillsdale, NJ: Scientific Software International. The WLS method was selected due to the mix of ordinal and continuous variables included in this study and due to the fact that several variables have skewed distributions.

36. Anhut & Heitmeyer. (2007).

37. Rohner et al. (2005).

38. For a review, see Agnew, R. (1995). Controlling delinquency: Recommendations from general strain theory. In H. D. Barlow (Ed.), *Crime and public policy* (pp. 43–70). Boulder, CO: Westview.

39. For example, Agnew. (1984); Moffit. (1993); Tittle. (1995). Also see Jacobs. (1999); Jacobs & Wright. (1999).

40. Chodorow, N. (1978). *The reproduction of mothering.* Berkeley: University of California Press; Gilligan, C. (1982). *In a different voice.* Cambridge, MA: Harvard University Press; Jacobs. (1999); Marwell. (1966); Matza, D. (1964). *Delinquency and drift.* Hoboken, NJ: Wiley.

41. Eccles et al. (1991); Murphey et al. (1963).

42. Jacobs. (1999); Moffitt. (1993); Tittle. (1995).

43. Jacobs & Wright. (1999); Shover & Honaker. (1992).

44. Felson, M. (1998). *Crime and everyday life* (2nd ed.). Thousand Oaks, CA: Pine Forge.

TIMOTHY BREZINA *is associate professor of criminal justice at Georgia State University in Atlanta.*

*In a multicultural society, assimilation is not the best path to social adjustment. A strong identity, from either the old culture or the new one or both, serves as a source of recognition and a buffer against violence. Marginalization seems to be the most damaging mode of adjustment.*

# 8

# Social identity and violence among immigrant adolescents

*Gustavo S. Mesch, Hagit Turjeman, Gideon Fishman*

FOR MANY YEARS, FOLLOWING Emile Durkheim's work, sociological and criminological theories have claimed that the weakening of social institutions and controls is at the root of antisocial behavior and that violence is only one of its manifestations. Social disintegration is a result of a weakening of social solidarity. According to Durkheim, rapid social change can cause uncertainty and anomie if traditional norms fail to serve as formal or informal social structures and are unable to maintain solidarity, stability, trust, and continuity.[1]

According to Anhut and Heitmeyer, social integration and disintegration can be separated into three dimensions: the macrolevel refers to access to labor and housing markets, the mesolevel to the

NEW DIRECTIONS FOR YOUTH DEVELOPMENT, NO. 119, FALL 2008 © WILEY PERIODICALS, INC.
Published online in Wiley InterScience (www.interscience.wiley.com) • DOI: 10.1002/yd.277

degree of citizens' participation in political and social institutions, and the individual level to the societal recognition of a person's group and unique personal identity.[2] Our study focuses on two of these aspects: perceived discrimination, which represents a person's perceived opportunity structure, and group identity. It also examines family function, which according to the theory is central to the understanding of violent behavior.

The criminological literature has traditionally treated immigration as an abrupt and disruptive process.[3] It might lead to social disintegration as parents, traditional agents of socialization and social control, lose their status and become irrelevant. Conflicts between adolescents and parents emerge as a result of disagreement over adherence to the old group's values and norms, which often contradict the values dominant in the new culture.[4]

Trying to account for social disintegration, traditional theories pointed to the structural strain that prevented people from achieving the culturally prescribed goals.[5] Shaw and MacKay and Sutherland and Cressey drew attention to the social disorganization process that takes place in poor, multiethnic immigrant neighborhoods amid normative conflicts.[6] More recent theories added a sociopsychological dimension by indicating that adolescents experience difficulties with identity and social expectations, which place them under additional personal psychological strain.[7] This approach assumes the presence of a dominant mainstream in society, which is relevant to most of its members who seek recognition. Studies on the acculturation of immigrants have pointed to the conflict between the dominant norms of the absorbing society and the immigrant culture.[8] The conflict is likely to confuse juveniles and reduce the influence of their families as control and socializing agents. According to this approach, newcomers to such a society eventually assimilate and adopt the customs and beliefs of the dominant culture. But social homogeneity, especially in the Western world, is increasingly replaced by social diversity and pluralistic social structures that highlight problems of recognition and identity.

## *Identity*

There has been a common belief in immigrant-absorbing societies that the melting pot model is the preferred one despite its known hazards. The estrangement from the old culture and assumption of a new identity as a means of assimilation is affected by many hazards, such as alienation from the old social network and family conflicts, that often result in loss of parental control and can lead to undesirable influences by delinquent peers.

Replacement of the ancestral cultural heritage cannot happen instantly. Immigrant youth may be torn between the two dominant identities: that of the ancestral culture and that of the host society as represented by the peer group. Immigrant adolescents who aspire to join the mainstream culture may be rejected, and become disappointed and frustrated. However, new cultural norms and values are not necessarily adopted at the expense of rejection of the old identity. This argument brings into question the relevance of the concept of assimilation in a multicultural setting.

As Portes and Hao have documented, until the 1960s, there was strong intellectual support for the melting pot ideology that objected to the idea of immigrants' retaining their foreign customs and language, which were seen as inimical to the individual and society. The debate over bilingualism versus monolingual language adaptation is one example of the broader issue of identity.[9]

Bilingualism was believed to slow the process of assimilation, and retention of native languages was considered a sign of basic intellectual inferiority. A landmark study by Peal and Lambert proved the opposite.[10] Bilingual students outperformed monolingual students on almost all cognitive tests. Linguists and psychologists have repeatedly noted the association of fluent bilingualism with better cognitive performance in comparison with monolinguals in any language.[11] These findings suggest that fluent bilingualism is preferred not only because of its effect on cognitive development but also because it has a higher probability of maintaining social solidarity within the family and facilitating successful personal adjustment.

The closer individuals are to their family, the more likely they are to use their native language when communicating with parents and peers and less likely to adopt the local language.[12]

The option of favoring both languages rather than adopting one at the expense of the other is also available, indicating the adoption of a double identity, rooted in both the old and the new cultures.

Research has shown that ethnic identification often facilitates a better adjustment to the host society precisely because it allows the cultivation of a distinctive identity, which helps adolescents receive recognition, reduces intergenerational conflict, and guards against involvement in dangerous behavior that may be part of the local peer group culture.[13]

## Acculturative experiences

One important consequence of immigration is the individual and group experience of acculturation within a context of culturally pluralistic societies.[14] Berry suggested that two independent dimensions underlie the process of acculturation: individual links to the culture of origin and to the society of settlement.[15] These links can be manifested in several ways, including preferences for involvement (termed acculturation attitudes) in the two cultures and the behaviors that they prescribe. Berry et al. identified four levels of acculturation associated with different levels of stress: assimilation, separation, integration (or biculturalism), and marginalization.[16] According to Berry, individuals who are assimilated or marginalized appear to experience the greatest amount of stress because assimilation and marginalization create a situation in which a person is not anchored in any one culture.[17] Acculturative stress, found primarily among culturally marginal social groups, increases the risk of violence. Conversely, among individuals who can be classified as attached to their ancestral culture, the level of acculturative stress is often lower, and this serves as a protective factor.[18]

Studies have shown that a high score on acculturation efforts is linked to a high level of violence. This is attributed to the rapid process of acculturation that distances adolescents from their parents and heightens norm conflicts between adolescents and their parents and between adolescents and their immigrant peers.[19] This finding is consistent with the work of Berry, who argued that adolescents who have assimilated or were marginalized experienced the greatest amount of stress because assimilation and marginalization fail to ground a person within any one culture. Acculturative stress increases the risk of violent behavior as a reaction to lack of recognition, perceived discrimination, and social isolation. A comparative study of adolescents from thirteen countries found that individuals who reported low ethnic identity and low language proficiency (in the new language) and scored low on the new social identity (marginalized) also showed poor psychological and school adaptation[20] and ran the risk of substance abuse and risk taking.[21]

## Perceived discrimination

In immigrant societies, those who are native born are often suspicious of new immigrants, who are perceived as reluctant to adopt the local culture, language, and customs. The local population may react to signs of unwillingness to assimilate rapidly with differential treatment of the immigrants.[22] Immigrants are not oblivious to such treatment and describe such experiences as discriminatory. Perceived discrimination is defined as a belief that one is treated unfairly because of one's origin.[23] In a sense, discrimination shows the lack of congruence between the immigrants' and the receiving society's orientations and expectations of each other.[24]

Perceived discrimination is considered a negative life event and a source of chronic stress, which may affect the immigrant's adjustment to the new society.[25] It can evoke feelings of anger and frustration, which may be released as violent behavior. Some studies found such experiences to be particularly detrimental to adolescents, negatively affecting their perceived efficacy, attitudes toward school, and school attainments.[26]

According to Anhut and Heitmeyer's disintegration theory, lack of recognition increases the likelihood of disintegration, motivating deviant behavior. This is not unique to immigrants; it also occurs in many other groups.[27] In any study of immigrants, lack of recognition should be perceived in its broadest structural and institutional sense as blocked opportunities to succeed, achieve status, and successfully adapt to the new society. However, with regard to acculturation and recognition, in the Western world in particular, acculturation and recognition take place in societies that have transformed into or are in the process of becoming multicultural entities. This gives new meaning to the question of the source of that recognition and what proper acculturation means.

---

## Family functioning

Delinquent adolescent behavior among immigrants has often been attributed to conflicts between family and children. One source of conflict is rooted in intergenerational gaps as parents retain their traditional values while adolescents adopt new values acquired in the new country.[28] This can lead to increased family conflicts and parent-child alienation, which can lead to a decline in family cohesion.[29] At the same time, where there are close relationships between parents and adolescents and family bonds remain intact, the family can ameliorate the negative effects of the stress of acculturation on adolescents. Parents can provide social support when their children are coping with adjustment problems in a new school or with possible frustration and anxiety as they try to join a new peer group.[30] Strong family bonds also protect adolescents from exposure to deviant peers and involvement in deviant acts. Family cohesion, even under conditions of acculturative stress, is able to monitor, regulate, and protect adolescents through direct intervention that shields youths from negative peer influences and abuse.

One of the characteristics associated with family malfunctioning is a decrease in monitoring and the drift of adolescents into unsupervised peer-oriented leisure activities. In such contexts, the likelihood of delinquent conduct becomes more likely.[31]

The rest of this article focuses on Israeli society, which from its inception has been an immigrant society, and examines the effect of these factors on immigrants' adjustment.

## Immigration to Israel

In Israel, the melting pot model of adjustment has become irrelevant not by choice but as a result of the wave of immigration that started in 1990 and continued for over a decade and a half. Arriving from the former Soviet Union (FSU) in large numbers, immigrants developed the feeling that maintaining their language, culture, remedial educational system, and other institutions, like theaters and orchestras, is legitimate and does not harm their integration into the mainstream of Israeli society. Thus, immigrant adolescents in Israel did not have to deny their Russian cultural roots and identity as they were striving to acquire an additional Israeli one. They were able to enjoy the advantages of successful integration into the new society and at the same time maintain their social ties with family and friends from the FSU.

In practice, the dual identity and integration pattern is manifested by a number of examples: immigrant adolescents volunteer to join elite units in the military, youth communicate in Russian without feeling awkward or uncomfortable, and physicians and heads of medical units in hospitals issue instructions in Russian to immigrant nurses without uneasiness or apology. At the same time, native-born Israelis learn to accept that being an immigrant, speaking one's native language, or maintaining a dress code common in the country of origin does not necessarily mean inferior status or lack of respect toward the dominant society. In other words, a multicultural society recognizes the right to be different.

The study examined here challenges the traditional approach to social disintegration, which finds the melting pot model useful to account for violence among adolescent immigrants. The research investigates what accounts for violence and delinquency among immigrant youth and whether adopting a new identity is associated with normative social adjustment.

## Data and methods

The study examined here is based on a national three-wave, face-to-face survey, conducted between 2002 and 2005, among 1,420 adolescents (ages twelve to eighteen) who immigrated from the FSU to Israel during the years 1997 to 2003. For the purpose of data collection, Israel was divided into three regions—north, central, and south—and thirteen towns with high concentrations of immigrants from the FSU were randomly selected: five in the north, five in the center, and three in the south. In each town, a quota was determined according to criteria of age, length of residence in Israel, gender, and country of origin. Face-to-face interviews were conducted in Russian without the presence of parents. After the third wave, the parents of the young people were interviewed in order to gain more information about them and the family and also to verify some of their children's responses. This study pertains to the third wave, by which the sample had shrunk to 910 youth.

### Study variables

*Dependent variables.* We used two conceptualizations of violent behavior (which refers only to physical violence). *Eclectic violence* refers to violent conduct in conjunction with other forms of delinquent acts (property or drug offenses). This variable was coded 1 if the adolescent had been involved in violent conduct as well as other forms of nonviolent delinquency and 0 when the adolescent had not been involved in any type of delinquency. *Specialized violence* refers to situations in which youths had been exclusively involved in violent conduct (coded 1). If the adolescent had not been involved in any type of delinquency, including violence, a code of 0 was assigned.

***Independent variables.*** *Social identity* was measured by two items asking respondents to report the extent to which they felt Israeli and Russian. Responses to both items were on a six-point Likert scale, with higher values (4–6) indicating higher identification. Two dummy variables were created. A value of 0 was assigned to individuals who reported low identification and a value of 1 to those who reported higher identification. We combined the dummy variables to create four identification modes: (1) high Israeli and high Russian, (2) high Israeli and low Russian, (3) low Israeli and high Russian, and (4) low Israeli and low Russian.

*Feelings of Alienation* was a composite variable consisting of five items that identify adolescents' difficulties in relating to Israelis and express a sense of exclusion (Cronbach alpha = .88).[32]

*Perceived Discrimination* was a composite scale consisting of six items that assess the perceived frequency of the participants' recent exposure to unfair or negative treatment by the host society because of their ethnic background in different settings such as school and administrative offices (Cronbach alpha = .81).[33]

*Delinquent Peers* was a composite scale consisting of four questions about the number of delinquent peers with whom the adolescents associate. The delinquent or deviant behaviors of the delinquent peers included such acts as theft, participation in violent acts, and property offenses (Cronbach alpha = .82).

*Family Functioning* was a composite scale consisting of eight items measuring joint family activities, willingness to listen to the adolescent, getting along with each other, parents' awareness of their adolescent's whereabouts, persons with whom the youths socialize, how the youths spend their money, where they spend time with friends at night, where they go, and what they do after school (Cronbach alpha = 90).

*Unsupervised Leisure Activities* was a composite scale based on four items that refer to the adolescents' pattern of spending leisure time in unsupervised activities such as discotheques, parties, rock concerts, and pool halls (Cronbach alpha = 66).

*Language Usage* was a four-item scale designed to measure the use of the Hebrew language. It measures the extent to which adolescents used Hebrew to communicate with parents and friends, read books, and watch TV. Responses were given on a five-point Likert scale, with higher values indicating more extensive use than lower ones (Cronbach alpha = .86).

*Mother's Education* was measured in years of formal education. (The correlation between the parents' education was very high. In order to avoid multicollinearity, mothers' education was used.)

*Length of Residence in the Country* was measured in months since arrival in Israel. The adolescent's age was measured in years, and gender was a dummy variable coded 1 for boys and 0 for girls.

### Sample description

The mean age of the study population was 15.7 years. The adolescents had been in the country for 5.4 years on average; 54 percent were males and 46 percent females. Fathers had an average of 13.6 years of schooling and mothers 13.9 years. As only 7 percent had one or both parents unemployed, the immigrant families seem to have integrated well into the Israeli labor market. In these families, 62.3 percent of parents were living together, 26.7 percent were divorced, 4.1 percent were separated, and 6.8 percent were widowed. When interacting with parents, adolescents used Hebrew less often than they did when interacting with friends: 52.1 percent of adolescents reported never using Hebrew in communicating with their parents, and 13 percent reported never using Hebrew in communicating with friends. In addition, 48.5 percent of respondents reported that the economic situation of the family had not changed as a result of immigration, 9.8 percent indicated that their economic situation had improved, and 41.7 percent reported that conditions had worsened.

As to violence, 16.4 percent of the study population reported involvement in eclectic violence and 9.2 percent in specialized violent conduct. Overall, 25.6 percent of the immigrant adolescents were involved in different types of delinquency.

## Results

When acculturation is examined in the context of social disintegration, identity becomes a main focus of the analysis. Because adaptation to the new culture is carried out in a multicultural context, the issue of identity is examined not on a one-dimensional scale, where one end of the scale represents the old identity and the other end the new identity, but on two separate scales: one for the Russian identity and the other for the new Israeli one. Our objective was to examine the association between self-reported identity and violent conduct. Table 8.1 presents the rate of involvement in violent behavior by categories of social identity.

In the case of eclectic violence, Table 8.1 shows that individuals who reported at least one high identity had a significantly higher probability of not being involved in eclectic violence than individuals with low Israeli and low Russian identity ($\chi^2 = 23.124$, $p < .01$). But this was not found when comparing normative with those involved in specialized violence. This could also indicate that specialized violence might not be associated with social disintegration,

Table 8.1. Distribution of social identity according to involvement in violent behavior

| | Eclectic violence (N) | Normative adolescents (N) | Specialized violence (N) |
|---|---|---|---|
| High Israeli/high Russian identity | 27% (48) | 130 | 15.9% (39) |
| Low Israeli/low Russian identity | 52% (26) | 24 | 18.1% (13) |
| High Israeli/low Russian identity | 29% (18) | 44 | 13.4% (11) |
| Low Israeli/high Russian identity | 45.6% (155) | 185 | 16% (78) |
| N | 247 | 383 | 141 |
| Chi square (df 7) | 23.124* | | .631 |
| Cramer C | .192* | | .027 |

*$p < .01$.

**Table 8.2. Mean differences in background variables (*t* test) for immigrants involved in eclectic violence**

| Variable | Normative adolescents | Eclectic violence |
|---|---|---|
| Age | 17.82 | 17.75** |
| | (1.91) | (1.71) |
| Gender[a] (1 = male) | .35 | .72* |
| | (.47) | (.44) |
| Mother's education[a] | .67 | .54** |
| | (.46) | (.49) |
| Length of residence in months | 61.95 | 67.25 |
| | (.18) | (18.87) |
| Perceived discrimination | −.30 | .54** |
| | (.89) | (1.76) |
| Use of language | .060 | −.19** |
| | (.97) | (.98) |
| Family functioning | .37 | −.48** |
| | (1.25) | (1.27) |
| Delinquent peers | −.42 | .68** |
| | (.38) | (1.38) |
| Leisure activities | −.148 | .272** |
| | (1.052) | (.895) |

[a]Refers to proportions.

*$p < .01$. **$p < .05$.

but rather with other variables that are not necessarily related to acculturation to the new society.

A *t* test was performed to determine whether there were significant differences in the means and proportions of the study variables. Table 8.2 indicates some statistically significant differences between eclectic violent youths and normative youths. The eclectic violent group was younger, composed of proportionally more males, and mothers' education was lower. Adolescents who reported involvement in eclectic violence had been in the country for a longer period than the normative youths had. The eclectic violent adolescents also reported a higher rate of negative encounters with the host society, as is evident from the significantly higher mean scores of perceived discrimination. They also reported less frequent use of the Hebrew

**Table 8.3. Mean differences in background variables (*t* test) for immigrants involved in violence only**

| Variable | Normative adolescents | Specialized violence |
|---|---|---|
| Age | 17.90 | 17.20** |
| | (1.89) | (1.71) |
| Gender[a] (1 = male) | .37 | .62** |
| | (.47) | (.48) |
| Mother's education[a] | .65 | .60 |
| | (.46) | (.49) |
| Length of residence in months | 63.04 | 63.85 |
| | (18.53) | (19.73) |
| Perceived discrimination | −.30 | .06** |
| | (.89) | (1.24) |
| Use of language | .019 | −.021 |
| | (.97) | (.96) |
| Family functioning | .23 | .033 |
| | (1.29) | (1.20) |
| Delinquent peers | −.32 | −.06** |
| | (.53) | (.79) |
| Leisure activities | −.14 | .06* |
| | (1.03) | (.93) |

[a]Refers to proportions.

*$p < .01$. **$p < .05$.

language than the normative adolescents. Their relationships with salient social groups appeared to be troubled, and they also reported lower levels of parental control and larger numbers of delinquent friends than did normative adolescents.

Next, we examined the differences in means and proportions between adolescents who were involved exclusively in violent behavior (specialized violence) and normative adolescent immigrants. In Table 8.3, as in Table 8.4, violent and normative immigrant adolescents differed in their age and gender characteristics. Immigrant adolescents involved in specialized violence were younger, and the proportion of males among them was higher.

A comparison of Tables 8.2 and 8.3 also reveals differences between eclectic and specialized violent youths. The use of

**Table 8.4. Logistic regression examining the effect of independent variables on eclectic violence relative to normative adolescents**

| | Parameter estimate (SE) | Odds ratio |
|---|---|---|
| Gender | 1.295k** (.278) | 3.652 |
| Age | −.028 (.080) | 1.028 |
| Low Israeli/low Russian identity | 1.113* (.533) | 3.043 |
| High Israeli/low Russian identity | −.164 (.596) | 1.177 |
| Low Israeli/high Russian identity | .192 (.331) | 1.212 |
| High Israeli/high Russian identity | — | — |
| Discrimination | .354** (.109) | 1.425 |
| Language use | −.267 (.162) | 1.305 |
| Length of residence | .015* (.008) | 1.015 |
| Mother's education | −.406 (.281) | 1.499 |
| Family functioning | −.315** (.112) | 1.369 |
| Delinquent peers | 1.849** (.259) | 6.356 |
| Leisure activities | .473** (.148) | 1.606 |
| Constant | −.1.303 (1.445) | 3.676 |
| Chi square | 248.046 | |
| −2 log likelihood | 347.596 | |

$*p < .01.$ $**p < .05.$

Hebrew is not statistically significant and does not predict either type of violent behavior. The same is true for family functioning (parental monitoring and family cohesion). However, in the case of eclectic violence and in specialized violence, those adolescents are likely to associate with delinquent peers and to participate in more unsupervised leisure activities than normative adolescents.

## Multivariate analysis

To determine whether the association of social identity and perceived discrimination with violent behavior holds true when other variables are controlled, we conducted a logistic regression analysis.

First, we compared eclectic violent adolescents with normative ones. The results (Table 8.4) show several variables that seem to increase the likelihood of eclectic violent behavior among immigrant adolescents. As expected, there are clear gender differences: females are less likely to be involved in eclectic violent behavior than males are. Social identity was also found to be statistically significant, which suggests that individuals with strong Israeli and Russian identities simultaneously (the omitted category) are less likely to be involved in eclectic violent behavior than those reporting low Israeli *and* Russian identities. Table 8.4 also shows that proper family functioning reduces the likelihood of eclectic violent behavior, whereas the probability of such behavior increases with an increase in the number of delinquent friends.

Additional variables that increased the likelihood of eclectic violence were length of residence and feelings of discrimination. Use of the Hebrew language was not found to be statistically significant in affecting eclectic violence.

Family functioning, a scale that jointly represents perceived family cohesion and parental monitoring, is negatively associated with the likelihood of violent behavior. By contrast, the higher the number of delinquent friends and the more one was involved in unsupervised leisure activities, the higher the likelihood is of eclectic violence.

Next, we checked whether the variables that affected eclectic violence maintained their significance when examining specialized violence as the dependent variable. Table 8.5 shows the results of a logistic regression model predicting the likelihood of involvement in specialized violent behavior.

The comparison between results affecting eclectic and specialized violence shows that the models are quite different, which supports and validates the decision to differentiate between the two forms of violence. In the model referring to specialized violence,

**Table 8.5. Logistic regression examining the effect of independent variables on specialized violence relative to normative adolescents**

|  | Parameter estimate (SE) | Odds ratio |
| --- | --- | --- |
| Gender | 1.231** | 3.426 |
|  | (.233) |  |
| Age | −.169* | 1.184 |
|  | (.065) |  |
| Low Israeli/low Russian identity | .434 | 1.544 |
|  | (.488) |  |
| High Israeli/low Russian identity | .215 | 1.240 |
|  | (.436) |  |
| Low Israeli/high Russian identity | .113 | 1.120 |
|  | (.271) |  |
| High Israeli/high Russian identity | — | — |
| Discrimination | .171 | 1.186 |
|  | (.103) |  |
| Language use | −.014 | 1.014 |
|  | (.136) |  |
| Length of residence | .005 | 1.005 |
|  | (.006) |  |
| Mother's education | −.106 | 1.111 |
|  | (.238) |  |
| Family | −.023 | 1.023 |
|  | (.095) |  |
| Delinquent peers | .601** | 1.824 |
|  | (.169) |  |
| Leisure activities | .274** | 1.316 |
|  | (.112) |  |
| Constant | 1.124 | 3.078 |
|  | (1.179) |  |
| Chi square | 84.154 |  |
| −2 log likelihood | 357.734 |  |

*$p < .01$. **$p < .05$.

only criminogenic variables reached statistical significance, while none of the variables that can be related to immigration reached the required level of statistical significance. Thus, results show that the younger the adolescent, the higher the probability of being involved in specialized violence, and also that adolescent males are more likely to be involved in this specialized violent behavior than are females. Moreover, association with delinquent peers and participating in unsupervised activities increase the likelihood of engaging in specialized violent behavior.

Acculturation variables did not gain statistical significance in the specialized violence model. These variables (social identity, perceived discrimination, language use, and length of stay in the country) were associated with eclectic violent conduct, indicating that being involved in specialized violent behavior is not associated with a process of social disintegration. Hence, it is plausible that specialized violence might be related to early childhood developmental processes and factors other than acculturation.

## *Discussion*

The terms *social solidarity, integration,* and *disintegration* were useful concepts in a world of homogeneous social entities, where social norms were a unifying power and social solidarity was the expected state of social being. In such societies, sudden changes due to economic crises, waves of immigration, or wars served a disruptive function that brought about strain, social disorganization, and even the collapse of social institutions in charge of maintaining solidarity, integration, and social order. But this picture seems to describe an old world that ceased to exist shortly after the end of World War II. Currently, nation-states are becoming increasingly heterogeneous, with massive waves of immigration significantly changing the culture, ethnic structure, and population composition of many countries.

Multiculturalism is characterized not only by ethnic diversity but also by diversity in customs, languages, and religions. While the melting pot model of a highly homogeneous society held through the middle of the twentieth century, Western societies today show a relatively low level of social solidarity, face problems in creating and maintaining symbols of national unity, and exhibit high social diversity.

In the light of such changes, we must question the old perception that links processes of acculturation with deviance and ask whether this view is relevant at all to understanding current social processes that link immigration with delinquency.

Following Angell, who claimed that the heterogeneity of a population is negatively related to its degree of social integration, other research has shown that geographical mobility (migration) is related to weak social integration and is associated with breakdowns in relational structures, resulting in higher crime rates.[34] Haynie and South suggest that perhaps one reason why mobility is linked to adolescent violence is because newcomers are especially likely—at least in the short-term—to be integrated or accepted into peer groups whose members encourage deviant, nonconforming or otherwise problematic behaviors.[35] Consistent with this argument, our study shows that adolescents who associated with delinquent peers were more likely to be involved in both types of violent conduct. Association with peers is motivated by the need for recognition and social status. However, whether the association is with fellow immigrants or native-born adolescents, with delinquent or normative youths, depends on the person's opportunity structure.

Lack of recognition is a key variable in explaining youth violence.[36] When recognition is not granted, the individuals may feel discriminated against due to their immigrant status. Our findings show that under certain conditions (such as lack of Russian or Israeli identity or poor family functioning), there is a strong association between feelings of discrimination and violence. It is likely that feelings of discrimination are a result of realizing that opportunities are blocked. These feelings are a source of frustration and anger, expressed at times through aggressive and violent conduct.

In a culturally, ethnically, and religiously heterogeneous society, recognition can also be achieved through alternative means. For individuals who maintain their ancestral identity and have alternatives for status achievement and recognition, the native culture is less crucial. Thus, the issue of acceptance and recognition becomes a question of recognition by whom. In a multicultural, pluralistic society, the answer is complex because the social structure may involve recognition by more than one group.

This article has examined the link between the acculturation of immigrant youths and violence. Accordingly, acculturation contains three major elements: family functioning, identity of the adolescent, and the adolescent's perception of the opportunity structure. Traditionally, family stress due to immigration and poor family functioning as a control agent, intergenerational conflicts that challenge parental authority, and downward mobility have been considered indicators for social disintegration and have been closely associated with violence, as shown in our findings.

In a multicultural society, we expect individuals to adopt more than one cultural identity. The common assumption has been that social disintegration is a state in which one's identification with the ancestral culture is weak and at the same time identification with the native culture is also lacking. Under such conditions, one supposedly is unable to adhere to a consistent system of values and will show signs of anomie. Our findings indicate that the ability of an individual to adopt at least one salient identity reduces the likelihood of violence, and youths who failed to adopt either an Israeli or a Russian identity were most likely to be involved in violence.

The association between cultural identity and disintegration must be contextualized in the light of rapid social changes that have created multiculturalism and a situation in which multiple identities are possible. Disintegration is therefore no more a result of poor internalization of the dominant culture than the inability to identify with either the ancestral or the native culture.

## Notes

1. Morenoff, J. D., Sampson, R. J., & Raudenbush, S. W. (2001). Neighborhood inequality, collective efficacy and the spatial dynamics of urban violence. *Criminology. 39*, 517–560.

2. Anhut, R., & Heitmeyer, W. (2006). *Disintegration, recognition and violence.* http://a.dorna.free.fr/RevueNo9/Rubrique2/R2SR1.htm

3. Sellin, T. (1938). Cultural conflict and crime. *American Journal of Sociology, 44*(1), 97–103.

4. Patterson, G. R., & Stouthamer-Loeber, M. (1984). The correlation of family management practices and delinquency. *Child Development, 55*, 1299–1307; Szapocznik, J., & Kurtines, W. M. (1993). Family psychology and cultural diversity. *Hispanic Journal of Behavioral Sciences, 48*, 400–407.

5. Merton. R. K. (1957). *Social theory and social structure* (Rev. and enl. ed.). New York: Free Press; Sellin, T. (1938). Cultural conflict and crime. *New York American Journal of Sociology*, *44*(1), 97–103; Cloward, R. A., & Ohlin, L. E. (1960). *Delinquency and opportunity: A theory of delinquent gangs.* New York: Free Press.

6. Shaw, C. R., & MacKay, H .D. (1969). *Juvenile delinquency and urban areas: A study of rates of delinquency in relation to differential characteristics of local communities in American cities.* Chicago: University of Chicago Press; Sutherland, E. H., & Cressey, D. R. (1970). *Criminology.* Philadelphia: Lippincott.

7. Agnew, R. (1992). Foundation for a general strain theory of crime and delinquency. *Criminology, 30*(1), 47–88.

8. Berry, J. W., Kim, U., Power. S., & Young, M. (1989). Acculturation attitudes in plural societies. *Applied Psychology International Review, 38,* 185–206.

9. Portes, A., & Hao, L. (2002). *The price of uniformity: Language, family, and personality adjustment in the immigrant second generation.* Working paper, Center for Migration and Development, Princeton University.

10. Peal, E., & Lambert W. E. (1962). The relation of bilingualism to intelligence. *Psychological Monographs, 76,* 1–23.

11. Cummins, J. (1976). Foundations of bilingual education and bilingualism. In C. Baker (Ed.), *Multilingual matters.* Bristol, UK; Hakuta, K., & Suben, J. (1985). Bilingualism and cognitive development. *Annual Review of Applied Linguistics, 6,* 35–45.

12. Phinney, J. S., Irma, R., Nava, M., & Huang, D. (2001). The role of language, parents and peers in ethnic identity among adolescents in immigrant families. *Journal of Youth and Adolescence, 30,* 135–153.

13. Bankston, C., & Min, Z. (1995). Religious participation, ethnic identification and adaptation of Vietnamese adolescents in an immigrant community. *Sociological Quarterly, 36,* 523–534; Wong, S. K. (1997). Delinquency of Chinese Canadian youth. *Youth and Society, 29,* 112–133.

14. Sam, D. L., & Berry, J. W. (2006). Introduction. In D. L. Sam & J. W. Berry (Eds.), *The Cambridge handbook of acculturation psychology.* Cambridge: Cambridge University Press.

15. Berry, J. W. (1997). Immigration, acculturation, and adaptation. *Applied Psychology, 46,* 5–34.

16. Berry, J. W., Kim, U., Power. S., & Young, M. (1989). Acculturation attitudes in plural societies. *Applied Psychology International Review, 38,* 185–206.

17. Berry, J. W. (1997). Immigration, acculturation, and adaptation. *Applied Psychology, 46,* 5–34.

18. Soriano, F., Lourdes, M., Rivera, K. Williams, J., Daley, S., & Rezink, V. (2004). Navigating between cultures: the role of culture in youth violence. *Journal of Adolescent Health, 34,* 169–176.

19. Wong, S. K. (1999). Acculturation, peer relations, and delinquent behavior of Chinese Canadian youth. *Adolescence, 34,* 108–119.

20. Berry, J. W., Phinney, J. S., Sam, D. L., & Vedder, P. (2006). Immigrant youth, identity and adaptation. *Applied Psychology: An International Review, 35,* 303–332.

21. Schwartz, S., Montgomery, M., & Briones, E. (2006). The role of identity in acculturation among immigrant people. *Human Development, 49*, 1–30.

22. Jackson, J. S., Williams, D., & Torres, M. (1997). *Perceptions of discrimination: The stress process and physical and psychological health.* Washington, DC: National Institute of Mental Health.

23. Berry, J. W., Phinney, J. S., Sam, D. L., & Vedder, P. (2006). Immigrant youth, identity and adaptation. *Applied Psychology: An International Review, 35*, 303–332.

24. Jasinskaja-Lahti, I., Liebkind, K., Horenczyk, G., & Schmitz, P. (2003). The interactive nature of acculturation: Perceived discrimination, acculturation attitudes and stress among young ethnic repatriates in Finland, Israel and Germany. *International Journal of Intercultural Relations, 27*, 79–97.

25. Taylor, J., & Turner, J. R. (2002). Perceived discrimination, social stress, and depression in the transition to adulthood: Racial contrasts. *Social Psychology Quarterly, 65*, 213–225.

26. Vega, W. A., & Rumbaut, R. (1991). Ethnic minorities and mental health. *Annual Review of Sociology, 17*, 351–383; Liebkind, K., Jasinskaja-Lahti, I., & Solheim, E. (2004). Cultural identity, perceived discrimination, and perceived parental support as determinants of immigrants' school adjustments: Vietnamese youths to Finland. *Journal of Adolescent Research, 19*, 635–656.

27. Anhut, R., & Heitmeyer, W. (2007). *Disintegration, recognition and violence.* http://a/dorna.free.fr/reviewno9/Rubrique2/R2SR1.htm.

28. Szapocznik, J., & Kurtines, W. M. (1993). Family psychology and cultural diversity. *Hispanic Journal of Behavioral Sciences, 48*, 400–407.

29. Phinney, J., Ong, A., & Madden, T. (2000). Cultural values and intergenerational value discrepancies in immigrant and non-immigrant families. *Child Development, 71*(2), 528–539.

30. Ge, X., Lorenz, F. O., Conger, R. D., Elder, G. H., & Simons, R. L. (1994). Trajectories of stressful life events and depressive symptoms during adolescence. *Developmental Psychology, 30*, 467–483; Meadows, S. O., Brown, J. S., & Elder, G. H. (2006). Depressive symptoms, stress and support: Gendered trajectories from adolescence to young adulthood. *Journal of Youth and Adolescence, 35*(1), 93–103.

31. Gil, A., Vega, W., & Dimas, J. (2006). Acculturative stress and personal adjustment among Hispanic adolescent boys. *Journal of Community Psychology, 22*, 43–54. Gonzales, N. A., Deardorff, J., Formoso, D., Barr, A., & Barrera, M. J. (2006). Family mediators of the relation between acculturation and adolescent mental health. *Family Relations, 55*, 318–330; Osgood, D. W., Wilson, J. K., O'Malley, P. M., Bachman, J. G., & Johnston, L. D. (1996). Routine activities and individual deviant behavior. *American Sociological Review, 61*, 635–655.

32. A regression method was used to calculate the factor scores. The scores are standardized and have a mean of 0 and a variance equal to the squared multiple correlations between the estimated factor scores and the true factor values.

33. Strobl, R., & Kühnel, W. (2000). *Dazugehörig und ausgegrenzt. Analysen zu Integrationsschancen junger Aussiedler.* München: Juventa-Verlag.

34. Angell, C. A. (1974). The moral integration of American cities. *American Journal of Sociology, 80*(3), 607–629; Crutchfield, R. D., Geerken, R., & Gove, W. R. (1982). Crime rate and social integration: The impact of metropolitan mobility. *Criminology, 20*(3–4), 467–478; Sampson, R., & Groves, W. B. (1989). Neighborhood structure and crime: Testing social disorganization theory. *American Journal of Sociology, 94*, 774–80.

35. Haynie, D. L., & South, S. J. (2005). Residential mobility and adolescent violence. *Social Forces, 84*(1), 361–374.

36. Heitmeyer, W. (1992). Desintegration und Gewalt. *Deutsche Jugend, 4,* 109–122.

GUSTAVO S. MESCH *is a professor of sociology at the University of Haifa, where he is also head of the Sociology Department and a senior research associate with the Center for the Study of Society.*

HAGIT TURJEMAN *is a research associate at the Center for the Study of Society at the University of Haifa.*

GIDEON FISHMAN *is a professor of sociology and criminology and a co-director of the Center for the Study of Society at the University of Haifa.*

*Turkish and Russian adolescents in Germany are much more violent than local Germans. The reason for this behavioral difference can be traced back to social disintegration and special cultural orientations.*

# 9

# Disintegration and violence among migrants in Germany: Turkish and Russian youths versus German youths

*Dirk Baier, Christian Pfeiffer*

THE ETHNIC DIVERSITY of children and youth in Germany today results from different migration waves that have taken place in Germany since its foundation in 1949. War refugees from Eastern Europe were followed by guest workers, particularly from Turkey, Yugoslavia, and southern Europe, during Germany's economic boom in the 1960s. In the 1980s and at the beginning of the 1990s, refugees from conflict areas and war zones, including Yugoslavia and Iraq, arrived in Germany. The last extensive migration wave in Germany arose from the collapse of the socialist states and the immigration of repatriates, mainly from the former Soviet Union and Poland. As was the case in the 1950s, the repatriates were of German origin. However, they had lived in other countries for forty or more years or grew up as children of repatriates in their home country. Thus, repatriates are not foreigners; they share the

NEW DIRECTIONS FOR YOUTH DEVELOPMENT, NO. 119, FALL 2008 © WILEY PERIODICALS, INC.
Published online in Wiley InterScience (www.interscience.wiley.com) • DOI: 10.1002/yd.278

same experience of migration accompanied by different physical, psychic, and social difficulties.

## Migration, disintegration, and socialization

The causes of violent behavior have long been a topic of criminological research.[1] Statistics show that non-Germans display criminal behavior to a greater extent than native Germans do.[2] In fact, the proportion of criminal offenses committed by foreigners is currently nearly double the proportion of this group in the total population. Suspects of Turkish origin represent nearly a fifth of all foreign suspects and thus form the largest group; Yugoslavian and Polish offenders form the second and third largest groups, respectively.

The findings of several studies are consistent with crime statistics: foreign youths, especially of southern European origin, report violent behavior more often than young Germans do.[3] The problem is that many of these studies may not report on results for different ethnic groups in a differentiated manner because of the low number of respondents. In addition, the results concerning repatriated adolescents are inconsistent. According to Naplava, repatriates are more often involved in thefts; at the same time, repatriates, in particular those from the former Soviet Union, show only slightly increased rates of violence. Babka von Gostomski, however, reports an increased propensity of violence for that group.[4]

The idea that migrants should show a higher willingness to commit criminal offenses is substantiated by at least three theoretical approaches. The theory of deprivation focuses on the social structural situation of the migrants. The initial point is that migrants in Germany are often disadvantaged because they seldom achieve higher levels of education and typically work in the low-wage sector. Several groups of migrants are affected by unemployment and payment of social benefits to a greater extent. Disadvantages in school and working life implicate that commonly shared cultural objectives may not be achieved in the institutionalized way established by society.

NEW DIRECTIONS FOR YOUTH DEVELOPMENT • DOI: 10.1002/yd

Cultural explanations focus on the existence and maintenance of specific orientations. In accordance with the theory of subculture, normative standards and values of a society do not apply to all social groups. Migrants do not break with the cultural convictions of their home country after migrating to Germany. Furthermore, the assumption is made that people even return to their original standards and value orientations, which may be opposed to the German ones, in answer to the lack of social integration.[5] A possible consequence is a clash of cultures, which may lead to violent behavior, particularly in adolescence.

The disintegration approach offers an additional explanation for higher crime rates among migrants.[6] It is based on the assumption that the objective of human action is to obtain acceptance and social appreciation. Both are enabled by integration in society and central social subsystems. In modern society, integration or disintegration in three domains is of particular importance: (1) the structural domain, which refers to the participation in material goods through access to the employment market and higher education; (2) the institutional domain, which refers to participation in political events; and (3) the socioemotional domain, that is, the domain of human relations.[7] People who are not accepted by the larger society experience this as a strain, which motivates actions to achieve integration.

In considering the German situation, the question arises as to whether disintegration can explain violence among young migrants. Because education in Germany is compulsory for nine years, and secondary and vocational education are widely available, adolescents between the ages of fourteen and eighteen are rarely in need of earning their own livelihood. In fact, their socioeconomic status is dependent on their parents' status. The same applies to the institutional dimension. Adolescents in Germany have limited opportunities to participate in political life; for instance, they are not eligible to vote until they are eighteen years old. Socioemotional disintegration, however, seems to be of high significance for all adolescents. The dissolution of old relations and the creation of new friendships is a central developmental task, so socioemotional disintegration is an experience typical for adolescents.

NEW DIRECTIONS FOR YOUTH DEVELOPMENT • DOI: 10.1002/yd

To examine integration dimensions relevant for adolescents, it seems reasonable to simultaneously consider the different domains of acceptance as well as socialization contexts. Socialization contexts in the sense of socioecological theory refers to all social systems where children are included and in which social values, normative standards, and behavior patterns obtain. The most important socialization contexts are family, school, and peer group. And it surely includes the media as well. If these contexts are divided into a more structural and a more socioemotional dimension, it is possible to specify the empirical indicators of integration and disintegration shown in Table 9.1. "Structural" means both the existence of access to a context (living together with parents or in a children's home, having or having no friends) and the status or position within the context. The socioemotional dimension may be divided into feelings (liking of parents and their parenting styles, liking of school) and cognitions (values socialized in family or peer group, knowledge learned in school).

Several studies have shown that some of the indicators in Table 9.1 are associated with higher violence rates among non-German adolescents. Wetzels et al. have demonstrated that the social status of non-German families is significantly worse than that of German families.[8] In addition, non-German families provide strain in emotional terms too. Wilmers et al. show that non-German adolescents are the victims of parental violence much more frequently than German adolescents are; this frequent con-

**Table 9.1. Indicators of disintegration divided into socialization contexts**

|  | Family | School | Peers | Media |
|---|---|---|---|---|
| Structural | Composition | — | Relations | Possession of technical devices |
|  | Social status | Type of school attended | Homogeneity/ heterogeneity | Duration of use |
| Socioemotional | Values | Academic performance | Group culture | Preferences for content |
|  | Parenting styles | Commitment to school | Shared leisure activities | |

frontation with parental violence results in more frequent imitation of them too.[9] Parenting styles are not independent of the parents' values, which they pass on to their children. Violence-related values are closely linked to juvenile violence. With reference to the "violence-legitimizing norms of masculinity," Enzmann et al. provide evidence that after controlling for these norms in multivariate models, no group of migrants turns out to be more violent than the German reference group.[10]

Because of Germany's compulsory school system, no difference between the youth groups exists with regard to school access. However, the type of school they attend is decisive. Job opportunities strongly depend on whether school is finished with a *Hauptschulabschluss* (the lowest school-leaving certificate in Germany) or the *Abitur* (highest school-leaving certificate). However, the type of school attended is only one part of school (dis)integration. In cognitive terms, school performance is important too; doing well in school may decrease the propensity to commit violent acts. School is also relevant in socioemotional terms: acceptance by teachers or integration into class results in a high commitment to school. Adolescents who have such a high commitment comply with school norms to a higher extent and rarely carry out violent acts.[11]

Disintegration may be observed in the field of peer group integration too. For instance, adolescents may differ regarding whether and how many close friendships they have. Existing friendships vary in many respects. For instance, studies by Haynie have shown that structural characteristics of peer networks are important determinants of deviant behavior.[12] It is assumed that ethnically homogeneous networks are particularly disadvantageous for migrants. Apart from the structural characteristics, the cultural aspect of the friendship network is important. According to the association hypothesis, contacts with delinquent friends increase the risk of becoming delinquent oneself. Typical leisure-time activities of these peer groups like hanging out create opportunities to commit delinquent acts. Oberwittler provides evidence that non-German girls and boys are members of a violent peer group to a significantly higher extent than German youth are.[13]

Today, however, leisure-time activities are increasingly media activities. A link between media use and violent behavior can be explained using different theoretical approaches. Empirical studies have verified that watching violent films and playing violent computer games is associated with juvenile violence.[14] The risk of watching such films and playing such games is significantly increased by the availability of appropriate devices and the intensity of use. For this reason, studies on media use should examine not only genres but also availability and length of use. So far, studies have found that non-German children show much higher rates of use, but the assumption that higher delinquency rates of non-German youths can be attributed to differential types of media use has not been systematically tested yet.[15]

Assumptions concerning the consequences of different forms of disintegration for violent behavior will be investigated in the following section using a large-scale school survey. The section presents results of descriptive analyses and conducts a multivariate analysis to determine whether disintegration explains a higher propensity for violence among non-German adolescents. All analyses are restricted to the two largest groups living in Germany, Turkish and Russian adolescents, which together represent more than two-fifths of all young migrants living in Germany.

## Sample description

The school survey examined here was conducted in the Old Federal States of Germany in 2005. It surveyed 14,301 adolescents, both boys and girls, in the ninth year of school (their average age was fifteen), in both large cities and districts. In some regions, complete surveys were carried out; thus, all students in their ninth year of school were interviewed; in other regions, samples were drawn, ensuring that at least every fourth student was surveyed. Except for special needs schools and the vocational preparation year, all types of schools are represented in the survey. It could not be ensured for all regions that the samples taken are an accurate representation of the population of students. For this reason, an adjustment weight (according to the type of school attended) has been constructed. We also refer to a survey conducted in 2006 with 3,661 ninth-year students in Hanover, which contains new instruments for measuring peer group integration.

To identify their background, the adolescents were asked to indicate their parents' nationality by birth in the questionnaire. If this nationality was Turkish, the student was classified as Turkish. If the father and mother were of different nationalities, the mother's origin was used for the classification. In case the father was not German and the mother was German, the youth was allocated to the corresponding non-German group. More than seventy nationalities were determined in this manner. The two largest groups are the Turkish (9.5 percent of all interviewed persons) and the Russian[16] (5.4 percent) interviewees. Furthermore, there were students of Yugoslavian (3.9 percent), Polish (3.5 percent), and Italian origin (2.2 percent); 11.6 percent of the interviewed ninth graders were of another non-German origin.

Table 9.2 presents information on how long the adolescents of the different groups had been living in Germany, how many were German citizens, and how large the proportion of binational parent combinations was. Turkish and Russian students formed two opposite groups: whereas 87.0 percent of the first group were born in Germany and 37.7 percent of them are of German nationality, only 10.6 percent of the Russian students were born in Germany; however, their origin was mostly German in the majority of cases because

**Table 9.2. Migration status by ethnic origin (weighted data)**

| Group | Born in Germany | In Germany for more than ten years | In Germany for less than ten years | German nationality | One German parent |
|---|---|---|---|---|---|
| German | 99.5% | 0.3% | 0.1% | 100.0% | 0.0% |
| Turkish | 87.0 | 7.8 | 5.3 | 37.7 | 8.2 |
| Russian | 10.6 | 31.6 | 57.8 | 85.0 | 9.0 |
| Other | 74.5 | 15.3 | 10.2 | 66.9 | 40.2 |
| Total | 88.3 | 5.9 | 5.8 | 86.2 | 9.8 |

NEW DIRECTIONS FOR YOUTH DEVELOPMENT • DOI: 10.1002/yd

of their repatriate background. More than half of the Russian adolescents had been in Germany for fewer than ten years. And only one
in eleven Turkish and Russian adolescents has a German parent.

---

## Disintegration and violence

### Violent behavior of German and non-German adolescents

To measure violent behavior, students were asked whether, and if yes,
how often they had committed bodily harm, a robbery, an extortion,
or held someone at gunpoint in the last twelve months. Because these
forms of physical violence are to a large extent a male phenomenon,
we restrict the analysis for a moment to all male persons interviewed.
All four behaviors were displayed much less frequently by German
adolescents (Table 9.3). Every fifth German male committed bodily
harm in the past year (19.1 percent), compared to almost twice as often
among Turkish males (37.5 percent). Russian and "other" males, too,
turn out to be significantly more violent regarding bodily harm.[17]

### Descriptive results on disintegration of non-German adolescents

*Family.* Two-thirds of the German students are currently living in a two-parent household (69.0 percent), compared to 84.3
percent of the Turkish and 73.3 percent of the Russian students.

**Table 9.3. Violence by ethnic origin, male interviewees only (weighted data)**

| Group | Bodily harm | Robbery | Holding someone at gunpoint | Extortion | At least one violent act |
|---|---|---|---|---|---|
| German | 19.1% | 3.2% | 2.7% | 1.1% | 20.7% |
| Turkish | 37.5 | 7.7 | 5.5 | 2.9 | 38.7 |
| Russian | 31.0 | 7.3 | 4.6 | 2.7 | 34.0 |
| Other | 29.1 | 5.9 | 4.2 | 2.6 | 29.9 |
| Total | 23.6 | 4.4 | 3.4 | 1.7 | 25.1 |
| Cramers V | .149*** | .083*** | .055*** | .061*** | .144*** |

***p < .001.

German adolescents have experienced a separation or divorce of the natural parents twice as frequently as Turkish adolescents and also more frequently than Russian adolescents. Complete families with two parents should be able to better monitor their children's behavior and to immediately punish it if necessary. Because Turkish children more often grow up in two-parent families, they should exercise less delinquent behavior. There are two possible reasons that this is not the case. First, the parental styles that Turkish children are confronted with differ from the styles of parents of other children, mainly regarding the use of violence. Second, Turkish families are larger, so the parents have to monitor a larger number of children.

In addition, Turkish families have a low social status. The parents of 47.7 percent of the Turkish students have a school-leaving certificate not exceeding the Hauptschule; the same applies to only 13.1 percent of the German and 6.3 percent of the Russian students. The low Russian value results from the fact that the majority of parents graduated in the former Soviet Union, which required ten years of schooling. In addition, the disintegration of Turkish families is reflected in their job status: 11.5 percent of the Turkish parents are unemployed compared to only 3.1 percent of Germans (Russians also have an 11.5 percent rate).

The acceptance of violence in non-German families is reflected in a more frequent use of violence by parents. Among the Germans, 17.0 percent reported having suffered heavy corporal punishments or abuse; the reported rates were almost twice as high for Turkish adolescents (29.8 percent) and 25.4 percent of Russian adolescents.[18] In addition, 26.1 percent of the Turkish adolescents indicated that their parents laid violent hands on each other in the past twelve months; the same applies to only 6.2 percent of the German and 13.7 percent of the Russian parents. These differences in parental styles remain if we control for the social status of German and non-German families.

Everyday confrontation with violence as well as the lack of supervision results in reinforcement of personal values and characteristics that lead to higher delinquency. For instance, 23.7 percent of all Turkish boys approve of so-called violence-legitimizing norms of masculinity, and a further 56.8 percent approve of them to some extent. The proportion of Russian boys explicitly approving these norms amounts to 9.2 percent (Germans, 3.9 percent), and the rate for part approval is 64.7 percent (Germans, 40.0 percent). These norms have been measured by statements such as, "A real man is strong and protects his family" and "Woman and children have to obey the man as the head of the family."[19] Apart from certain values, self-control is influenced by parental styles as well. Turkish adolescents report an explosive and unstable temper the most frequently (17.8 percent); this is not as often the case for Russian and German adolescents (13.5 and 11.2 percent, respectively).[20]

*School.* The type of school attended is a decisive differentiation criterion for ethnic groups. At the time of the survey, 14.3 percent of German youths attended a Hauptschule and 38.7 percent attended a Gymnasium, compared to 42.9 percent and 11.6 percent, respectively, of the Turkish adolescents. However, school-leaving certificates are only one indicator of the lower cultural capital of non-German families. For example, only 36.5 percent of the Turkish compared to 45.1 percent of the Russian and 60.0 percent of the German adolescents visited a museum in the past twelve months. Only 14.3 percent of the Turkish compared to 57.1 percent of the German adolescents possess classical literature at home (Russians 44.5 percent). In Turkish households, the availability of books is poor: fifty or fewer books are available in 58.4 percent of Turkish households; the same applies to only 18.2 percent of the German households (Russians, 36.7 percent).

The cognitive and emotional aspects of school attendance do not vary much by ethnic group. As expected, non-German students earn lower grades in German than German students do, regardless of the type of school attended. This does not apply to grades in mathematics, however. In this subject, students of Russian origin have better grades than Germans and Turks, both of whom show similar performance. On the question about whether they like school (commitment to school), the students answered in much the same way: approximately two-thirds of them show a high commitment to school. The Turkish adolescents feel the most integrated in the class community and consider themselves to be accepted by teachers the most frequently.

*Peers.* In the 2006 Hanover survey, more than two-thirds of the adolescents reported that they have a circle of friends. Ethnic differences can be found only for female interviewees: Turkish girls are most rarely in such a group (64.1 percent) and German girls (75.8 percent) most often, with Russian girls at 72.8 percent. Russian adolescents have the largest circle of friends. Russian girls have on average 9.9 friends, Turkish girls 7.0, and German girls 7.9; Russian boys have 12.6 friends, Turkish boys 12.2, and German boys 9.8.

Turkish girls have the fewest male friends and Russian girls the most (Table 9.4). More than every fourth friend of a Russian girl but only every sixth friend of a Turkish girl is a boy. Furthermore, the boys who are friends of Russian girls are older than those of German and Turkish girls: three times more friends than among

**Table 9.4. Character of adolescents' friendship networks by ethnic origin and gender, Hanover, 2006 (weighted data)**

|  | Ethnic group | Proportion of boys | Proportion of youths older than age seventeen | Proportion of friends with the same ethnic origin[a] | Proportion of friends living in the same district |
|---|---|---|---|---|---|
| Girls | German | 24.3% | 6.0% | 83.8% (1.50) | 42.6% |
|  | Turkish | 17.0 | 7.4 | 52.6 (4.48) | 51.1 |
|  | Russian | 28.3 | 18.3 | 40.7 (4.49) | 42.4 |
| Boys | German | 85.6 | 5.1 | 81.2 (1.45) | 54.2 |
|  | Turkish | 94.6 | 5.2 | 53.4 (4.56) | 68.2 |
|  | Russian | 88.9 | 10.9 | 53.5 (5.90) | 58.9 |
| Total |  | 52.4 | 6.8 | 74.5 (2.30) | 49.5 |
| F-ratio girls/ boys |  | 5.329**/ 9.142*** | 22.181***/ 5.752** | 159.248***/ 60.758*** | 2.675/ 5.818** |

[a]The numbers in parentheses show the ratio of the proportion of friends with the same ethnic origin to the ethnic group's proportion of the population.

**p < .01. ***p < .001.

German or Turkish girls are eighteen years or older. With regard to boys, the gender-related homogeneity is considerably higher than for girls. The Turkish boys' networks of friendships are 95 percent boys. Again Russian boys often have more contact with older persons than boys of other ethnic origins.

Ethnic homogeneity, that is, the proportion of friends of the same ethnic origin, is highest among German youths: 83.8 percent of the German girls' friends and 81.2 percent of the German boys' friends are of German origin. In contrast, only 52.6 percent of the Turkish girls' friends and 53.4 percent of the Turkish boys' friends are of Turkish origin. These findings on ethnic homogeneity, however, do not consider the probability of establishing relationships with friends of the same ethnic origin. In Hanover, 55.8 percent of all adolescents were of German, 11.7 percent of Turkish, and 9.1 percent of Russian origin. If we take this into account, we find the lowest network homogeneity for German adolescents, regardless of their gender. The networks of Turkish and, above all, Russian adolescents seem to be much more homogeneous. In addition, Turkish adolescents show distinctive features. Two-thirds of the Turkish boys' friends live in the same district (68.2 percent) compared to 54 percent for German boys.

The culture of the peer group was measured by different items. Statements such as, "We don't care about legal regulations" or "My friends would even start a quarrel with the police" (six items, alpha = .85), indicate a delinquent culture. Both non-German girls and non-German boys more often belong to delinquent groups. Whereas only 5.8 percent of the German girls reported a delinquent culture for their group, the rate for Turkish girls was 15.0 percent and for Russian girls 12.2 percent. In addition, 16.7 percent of German boys, but 28.8 percent of Turkish and 30.0 percent of Russian boys, agreed with these statements.

*Media.* We found that the surveyed youth watch TV or a video or DVD on a usual school day for two hours and fourteen minutes, along with fifty-four minutes playing computer games and fifty-three minutes on the Internet. This adds up to four hours of media time. Gender-related differences mainly exist concerning computer games and Internet surfing: girls pursue both activities for 57 minutes each day, while boys do this for 158 minutes. All in all, ethnic differences are rather negligible.

By the time they are fifteen years old, adolescents are in the possession of technical devices (TV as well as computers or DVDs) to a rather same level and use them more or less for the same period of time, regardless of ethnic origin. But there are significant differences with regard to the adolescents' preferences for violent media genres. Whereas only 13.6 percent of German adolescents regularly play violent games, 29.6 percent of Turkish adolescents and 20.9 percent of Russian adolescents do. Horror films are preferred by 35.7 percent of German, 44.6 percent of Turkish, and 45.4 percent of Russian adolescents.

## *Conclusion*

Multivariate analyses allow investigating which disintegration indicators may best help to explain the higher violence rates of non-German adolescents. The results of these analyses are summarized in a final structural equation model (Figure 9.1), which refers to data from the 2005 survey. The analyses were carried out by means of AMOS.

Only variables have been included, measured as follows. For delinquent friends, the maximum value on friends—those who committed a bodily harm, robbery, shoplifting, car theft, car break-in, or drug dealing—was used. The variable was logarithmized by reason of its skewness. Self-control was measured by means of the temper dimension, norms of masculinity in accordance with the recommendation made by Enzmann et al. Violent media use was measured by the maximum value of watching horror and action films, as well as of playing Egoshooter and Beat-em-up games. Socioeconomic status is represented by ISEI88-values (International Socio-Economic Index of Occupational Status), following

# Figure 9.1. Model explaining the prevalence of violence

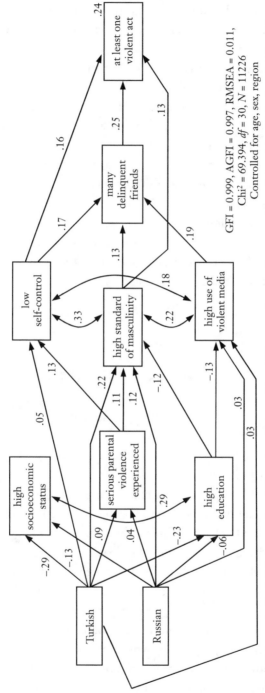

*Note:* Only standardized paths greater than .10 have been illustrated ($p < .001$), except for paths that connect the ethnic origin with further variables and are significant ($p < .01$). Goodness of Fit (GFI) = 0.999, Adjusted Goodness of Fit (AGFI) = 0.997, Root Mean Square Error of Approximation (RMSEA) = 0.011, chi square = 69.394, $df = 30$, $N = 11.226$. Controlled for age, sex, and region.

the recommendation of Albrecht et al.; parents without any job status (unemployed, housewife) have been assigned a 0.[21] Serious parental violence experienced in childhood consists of three items (beaten with an object, punching, beaten up); the highest violation frequency was encoded. Education is measured by estimated years of attending school (Hauptschule, nine years; Realschule, ten years; and Gymnasium, thirteen years).

Both non-German groups, but particularly Turkish adolescents, grow up with parents who have a lower socioeconomic status more frequently than Germans do. However, this has no consequence, which means that deprivation-theoretic explanations can be rejected at this point. A high or low status does not relate to other variables of the model. Educational level is an exception: parents with higher socioeconomic status often enable their children to have a higher education. Turkish adolescents are directly disadvantaged because this opportunity is provided to them much more seldom than to Germans; Russian adolescents are less disadvantaged compared to the German interviewees.

In turn, high education is an important factor in reducing the willingness to watch or play violent media genres and affirm violence-legitimizing norms of masculinity. These norms are the most important mediating factor in the model. Young Turks and Russians approve the norms of masculinity. In addition, young people who hold high norms of masculinity team up with delinquent friends more frequently and commit more violent offenses.

Parental violence constitutes a third central factor. Both non-German youth groups, but again especially Turkish adolescents, have reported serious parental violence more frequently than German adolescents. Other factors included in this model are less important for explaining ethnic differences in violent behavior. Although Turkish and Russian adolescents belong to the group of violent media users more frequently, the effects are rather negligible. Young people who engage with violent media frequently have a stronger affinity for norms of masculinity and try to get in touch with delinquent friends more often. Young Turks especially develop an unstable temper, particularly in confrontation with high family violence. Their low self-control relates to both their own violent behavior and their contact with delinquent friends.

The model in Figure 9.1 was calculated separately for the three ethnic groups. In all groups, parental violence leads to low self-control and a strong orientation toward norms of masculinity, which increases the probability of committing violent acts. High education reduces the orientation toward masculinity as well as the use of violent media for the Germans, Turks, and Russians. However, the separate models call attention to some particularities. First, the influence of norms of masculinity is rather low for young Turks, but the influence of parental violence is rather high. This is one reason to focus on changing parental styles of Turkish families. Second, among the Russian interviewees, the influence of education is lower than among German and Turkish interviewees. Strong determinants for violent behavior are low self-control and contact with delinquent peers. Both factors depend on parenting styles and media use.

On the basis of our theoretical approaches, we can conclude that ethnic differences in violent behavior do not result solely from objective deprivation experience; only the type of school attended turns out to be a factor, which relates to higher rates of violent behavior of non-German adolescents. Instead, the results point to cultural explanations. These may include both parenting styles and certain ideas on masculinity as products of a specific cultural environment. However, more than a pure migrants' culture is at play here. There are numerous non-German adolescents brought up without any household violence and who turn away from norms of masculinity and young Germans who experienced parental violence and internalized norms of masculinity. Future research should pay more attention to conditions supporting the formation of these specific violent cultures.

### Notes

1. Albrecht, H. J. (2001). Immigration, Kriminalität und Innere Sicherheit [Immigration, crime and inner security]. In G. Albrecht, O. Backes, & W. Kühnel (Eds.), Gewaltkriminalität zwischen Mythos und Realität [Violent crime between myth and reality] (pp. 259–281). Frankfurt am Main: Suhrkamp.

2. Pfeiffer, C., Kleimann, M., Petersen, S., & Schott, T. (2005). Migration und Kriminalität [Migration and crime]. Baden-Baden: Nomos.

3. Naplava, T. (2002). *Delinquenz bei einheimischen und immigrierten Jugendlichen im Vergleich.* [A comparison of delinquent behavior of native Germans and migrants]. Freiburg: Max-Planck-Institut.

4. Babka von Gostomski, C. (2003). Gewalt als Reaktion auf Anerkennungsdefizite? [Violence as a reaction to lack of recognition?]. *"Kölner Zeitschrift für Soziologie und Sozialpsychologie, 55,* 253–277.

5. Enzmann, D., Brettfeld, K., & Wetzels, P. (2004). Männlichkeitsnormen und die Kultur der Ehre [Norms of Masculinity and the culture of honour]. In D. Oberwittler, & S. Karstedt (Eds.), *Soziologie der Kriminalität* [Sociology of crime] (pp. 240–263). Wiesbaden: VS Verlag.

6. Babka von Gostomski. (2003).

7. Anhut, R., & Heitmeyer, W. (2000)."Desintegration, Konflikt und Ethnisierung [Disintegration, conflict and ethnicizing.]." In W. Heitmeyer & R. Anhut (ed.), *Bedrohte Stadtgesellschaften* [Threatened urban societies] (pp. 17–75). Weinheim: Juventa.

8. Wetzels, P., Enzmann, D., Mecklenburg, E., & Pfeiffer, C. (2001). *Jugend und Gewalt* [Youth and violence]. Baden-Baden: Nomos.

9. Wilmers, N., Enzmann, D., Schaefer, D., Herbers, K., Greve, W., & Wetzels, P. (2002). *Jugendliche in Deutschland zur Jahrtausendwende: Gefährlich oder gefährdet?* [Adolescents in Germany at the turn of the millennium: Dangerous or endangered?]. Baden-Baden: Nomos.

10. Enzmann et al. (2004).

11. Jenkins, P. H. (1997). School delinquency and the school social bond. *Journal of Research in Crime and Delinquency, 34,* 337–367.

12. Haynie, D. L. (2001). Delinquent peers revisited: Does network structure matter? *American Journal of Sociology, 106,* 1013–1057; Haynie, D. L., & Osgood, W. D. (2006). Reconsidering peers and delinquency: How do peers matter? *Social Forces, 84,* 1109–1130.

13. Oberwittler, D. (2003). Geschlecht, Ethnizität und sozialräumliche Benachteiligung [Gender, ethnicity and spatial disadvantage]. In S. Lamnek & M. Boatca (Eds.), *Geschlecht—Gewalt—Gesellschaft* [Gender—power—society] (pp. 269–295). Opladen: Leske + Budrich.

14. Anderson, C. A., & Bushman, B. J. (2001). Effects of violent video games on aggressive behavior, aggressive cognition, aggressive affect, physiological arousal, and prosocial behavior. *Psychological Science, 12,* 353–359.

15. Mössle, T., Kleimann, M., & Rehbein, F. (2007). *Bildschirmmedien im Alltag von Kindern und Jugendlichen* [Media in the life of children and adolescents]. Baden-Baden: Nomos.

16. The correct term would be "Russian/former Soviet Union," because this group also includes adolescents who originate from other former Soviet Union states.

17. Unless otherwise reported, in the following it may be assumed that the differences between the ethnic groups are significant at least at the 1 percent probability level.

18. Family violence experiences have been measured on the basis of the Conflict Tactic Scale. Cf. Straus, M. A. (1979). Measuring intrafamily conflict and violence: The Conflict Tactics (CT) Scales. *Journal of Marriage and*

*Family*, *41*, 75–88. Heavy corporal punishment or abuse means frequent slapping in the face, strong shaking, or hitting with an object or experiences with beating, punching, or beating with an object.

19. For all eight items and psychometric properties of the scale, see Enzmann et al. (2004).

20. Temper was measured on the basis of statements such as, "If I am really in conflict with someone, it is difficult for me to keep calm." Cf. Grasmick, H. G., Tittle, C. R., Bursik, J. R., & Arneklev, B. (1993). Testing the core empirical implications of Gottfredson and Hirschi's general theory of crime. *Journal of Research in Crime and Delinquency*, *30*, 5–29.

21. Albrecht, A., Trappmann, M., & Wolf, C. (2002). Statusmasse light: Statusskalen bei unzureichenden Berufsangaben. [Status measures light: Status scales despite insufficient occupational data]. *Kölner Zeitschrift für Soziologie und Sozialpsychologie*, *54*, 343–361.

DIRK BAIER *is a research associate at the Criminological Research Institute of Lower Saxony in Hanover, Germany.*

CHRISTIAN PFEIFFER *is professor of criminology, juvenile criminal, and correction at the University of Hanover, Germany, and director of the Criminological Research Institute of Lower Saxony.*

*Right-wing extremist violence is a complex phenomenon with different causes. From the perspective of social disintegration theory, right-wing extremist violence can be understood as a "productive" way of dealing with individual recognition deficits.*

# 10

# Right-wing extremist violence among adolescents in Germany

*Peter Sitzer, Wilhelm Heitmeyer*

RIGHT-WING EXTREMIST ORIENTATIONS are characterized by the confluence of ideologies of unequal worth and the acceptance of violence as a mode of action.[1] The devaluation of social minorities can be interpreted as a step on the road to a right-wing extremist orientation, especially where hostile attitudes coalesce with approval of and willingness to use violence. In the 2006 Group Focused Enmity (GFE) survey, 30.1 percent of interviewees agreed with xenophobic statements, 7.6 percent with racist statements, and 5.5 percent with anti-Semitic statements; 12.2 percent rejected homosexuals, 10.2 percent rejected the homeless, and 2 percent rejected disabled people; 34.1 percent demand precedent rights and 16.3 percent agreed with sexist statements.[2] Although approval of and willingness to use violence are much less widespread, these, like hostile attitudes, are found in all age groups.[3] Another representative population survey, also conducted in 2006, found clear approval

NEW DIRECTIONS FOR YOUTH DEVELOPMENT, NO. 119, FALL 2008 © WILEY PERIODICALS, INC.
Published online in Wiley InterScience (www.interscience.wiley.com) • DOI: 10.1002/yd.279

for certain right-wing extremist statements: 4.8 percent of respondents supported the idea of a right-wing authoritarian dictatorship, 19.3 percent agreed with chauvinist statements, 4.5 percent agreed with social Darwinist statements, and 4.1 percent played down the crimes of National Socialism.[4]

Of course, hostile attitudes, right-wing extremist orientations, and even approval of and willingness to use violence do not automatically lead to actual acts of violence. But the upward trend in right-wing extremist crime statistics and studies of crime suspects that we outline in the first section of this article suggest that the existence of these convictions in society helps to legitimize attitudes that become expressed in violence, in particular by adolescents and young adults. In the second section, we analyze the issue using a five-stage process model that portrays the underlying preconditions for acts of right-wing extremist violence, the contexts in which such violence takes place, and the factors that cause it to escalate. Using this structural model, we then outline central findings from German research about right-wing extremist violent offenders. For analytical reasons, the basic elements of the process model (socialization, organization, legitimation, interaction, and escalation) are treated separately, although together they form a whole. Finally, we examine right-wing extremist violence from the perspective of social disintegration theory.

## Trends in right-wing extremist crime in Germany

In 1991, one year after German reunification, right-wing extremist crime jumped to a level hitherto unheard of in postwar Germany. After a couple of years, it became clear that these right-wing extremist crimes were no temporary escalation connected with high numbers of asylum seekers. Figure 10.1 shows the development of right-wing extremist crime in various statistics of reported crime.[5]

Although the trends illustrated here must be interpreted with caution owing to several changes in statistical categories, it is clear that right-wing extremist crime rose steadily during the 1980s and jumped massively between 1991 and 1993. During the mid-1990s,

## Figure 10.1.  Right-wing extremist crime in Germany, 1980–2006

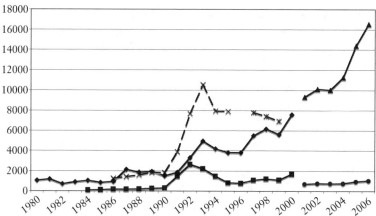

—♦— Right-wing extremist, xenophobic, and anti-Semitic crimes
—✱— Right-wing extremist offenses
—▲— Offenses with an extremist background in the field of "politically motivated crime—right-wing"
—✕— Violent and other offenses with a proven or suspected right-wing extremist background
—■— Violent offenses with a proven or suspected right-wing extremist background
—●— Violent offenses with an extremist background in the field of "political motivated crime—right-wing"

*Source:* Right-wing extremist, xenophobic, and anti-Semitic crimes, 1980 to 1992, West Germany; 1991 and 1992 including the whole of Berlin; since 1993. Germany: PKS-S. BMI/BMJ. (2001). *Erster periodischer Sicherheitsbericht.* Berlin. Right-wing extremist offenses: KPMD-S BMI/BMJ. (2001). *Erster periodischer Sicherheitsbericht.* Berlin. Offenses with an extremist background in the field of politically motivated crime—right wing: BMI. (2002, 2003, 2004, 2005, 2006, 2007). *Verfassungsschutzbericht 2001, 2002, 2003, 2004, 2005, 2006.* Berlin. Violent and other offenses with a proven or suspected right-wing extremist background: PKS-S. BMI. (1996). *Verfassungsschutzbericht 1995.* Berlin. Violent offenses with a proven or suspected right-wing extremist background, 1984–1990, West Germany; since 1991, Germany: PKS-S: BMI. (1984, 1985, 1995, 1997, 1998). *Verfassungsschutzbericht 1983, 1984, 1994, 1996, 1997.* Berlin. Violent offenses with an extremist background in the field of politically motivated crime—right wing: BMI. (2002, 2003, 2004, 2005, 2006, 2007). *Verfassungsschutzbericht 2001, 2002, 2003, 2004, 2005, 2006.* Berlin.

it decreased somewhat but remained clearly above the pre-1990 level. In the second half of the 1990s, right-wing extremist crime increased again, with violent right-wing extremist offenses reaching a second peak in 2000. The new definition system identifies considerably fewer violent right-wing extremist offenses and considerably

more other right-wing extremist offenses than the statistics for preceding years, with each year recording more violent and other
crimes than its predecessor. In relation to the population, the level
of right-wing extremist crimes in the eastern states (former East
Germany) has been fairly consistently above average since 1991.

### Which crimes are involved?

The category "politically motivated crime" (*Politisch motivierte
Kriminalität*) is used to record crimes reported to the police where
"the circumstances of the crime or the attitude of the suspect give
reason to believe that it was directed against a person on the
grounds of his or her political views, nationality, ethnicity, race, skin
color, religion, creed, origins, sexual orientation, disability, outward
appearance, or social status."[6]

   In 2006, 1,047 violent offenses were categorized as "politically
motivated crime, right wing" (Table 10.1). Of these, 484 were
xenophobic, 43 were anti-Semitic, 302 were directed against left-
wing extremists or supposed left-wing extremists, and 91 were
against other political adversaries. The remaining violent right-
wing extremist offenses were not assigned to any particular target.[7]

### Who are the offenders?

Official crime statistics provide few data concerning perpetrators
of violent right-wing extremist offenses. However, two analyses of
police files of suspects in xenophobic offenses (violent and other)
from Germany may give a review.[8] Both studies had similar results.
Most suspects are male adolescents between ages fifteen and
twenty-four. An above-average number of suspects have under—
average educational achievement and are more frequently affected
by unemployment or hold blue-collar jobs. More than three-
quarters of xenophobic offenses are committed by groups or individuals in a group context. Furthermore, about one-third were
suspects of earlier political offenses. The high proportion of suspects without previous convictions for political offenses and the
high proportion of group offenses point to a broad overlap between
xenophobic offenses and general youth and gang delinquency,

**Table 10.1.  Politically motivated right-wing extremist offenses, 2006**

|  | *Absolute* | *Percentage* |
|---|---|---|
| Violent offenses | | |
| Homicide | 0 | 0 |
| Attempted homicide | 2 | >0.1 |
| Bodily injury | 919 | 5.2 |
| Arson | 18 | 0.1 |
| Causing an explosion | 1 | >0.1 |
| Violation of the public peace | 33 | 0.2 |
| Endangering rail, air, water, or road transport | 6 | >0.1 |
| False imprisonment | 0 | 0 |
| Robbery | 13 | >0.1 |
| Blackmail | 7 | >0.1 |
| Resistance to public authority | 50 | 0.3 |
| Sexual offenses | 0 | 0 |
| Total | 1,047 | 5.9 |
| Other offenses | | |
| Property damage | 391 | 2.2 |
| Coercion or threat | 150 | 0.9 |
| Propaganda offenses | 12,627 | 71.8 |
| Disturbing the peace of the dead | 14 | >0.1 |
| Other offenses, in particular incitement to hatred | 3,368 | 19.1 |
| Total | 16,550 | 94.1 |
| Overall total | 17,597 | 100 |

*Source:* BMI. (2007). *Berfassungsschutzbericht 2006.* Berlin.

which from the perspective of anomie theory could be interpreted as an innovative adaptation to positional recognition deficits.[9]

Because police files tell us almost nothing about integration problems in other dimensions, we draw on sociological investigations of the preconditions for right-wing extremist violence, the contexts in which it takes place, and the factors that cause it to escalate.

### How do the offenses come about?

To answer this question, we draw on the SOLIE model (socialization, organization, political legitimation, interaction, escalation), shown in Figure 10.2.[10] This process model is based on socializing preconditions, which include individual learning of processes of violence and individual learning of hostile attitudes. Nevertheless,

**Figure 10.2.  The SOLIE model**

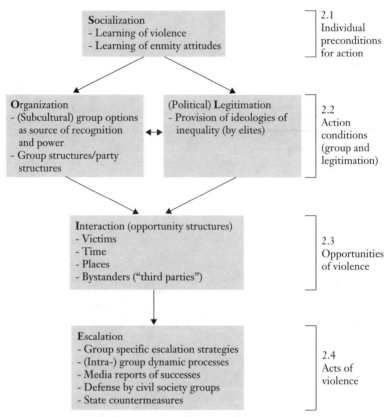

*Source:* Heitmeyer, W. (2003). Right-wing extremist violence. In W. Heitmeyer & J. Hagan (Eds.), *International handbook of violence research* (p. 411). Dordrecht: Kluwer.

as long as no public legitimation for violence or hostility is provided by elites and no organizations exist to provide opportunities for action or mobilization, these remain an individual and private matter. Relevance for action arises only when opportunity structures are present, that is, when interactions become possible that allow underlying attitudes and bases for action to escalate into violence.[11]

### Socialization: How the preconditions for action develop

One central source of right-wing extremist violence is found in specific socialization experiences. Here, socialization is understood as a process of appropriation of and interaction with the social and material conditions of life in a specific historical social context, in the course of which the biological human organism develops into a socially viable personality.[12] From this perspective, right-wing extremist convictions and advocacy of violence are seen as a product of the way a subject processes external reality in interaction with his or her internal reality. Neither the subject nor society is pathologized here; it is the interaction of individual and social factors that paves the way for developments that may appear extremely productive in the subject's internal logic—they may, for example, enhance his or her personal or social recognition—but are at the same time extremely destructive for society.[13] Although individual experiences in the family do not determine specific developments, they do represent the starting conditions for subsequent processes.[14]

In fact, with respect to family experiences linked to use of violence and willingness to use violence, violent right-wing extremist offenders do not differ greatly from other violent offenders unconnected with right-wing extremism.[15] Direct and indirect experience of violence, active humiliation, and passive denial of recognition stand at the beginning of "normal" careers of violence and of right-wing extremist careers of violence too, with such development trajectories being found disproportionately often among adolescents from broken families.[16] If right-wing extremist violence is a specific manifestation of the violence of adolescents, this leads us to the question of the origins of xenophobic attitudes and right-wing extremist ideologies.

The research group led by Hopf focuses in various investigations on the importance of parent-child attachment and the significance of the way adults deal with childhood attachment experiences for the development of right-wing extremist orientations in fifty-two young men and women.[17] An analysis of subjective representations of early attachment experiences showed that neither the young men nor the young women who represented their attachment experiences as "secure and autonomous" went on to develop right-wing extremist orientations.[18] And most of those who represented their attachment experiences as "dismissive/avoidant" or "preoccupied" had right-wing extremist orientatations.[19] In the interviews, the men and women with right-wing extremist orientations considerably more often reported having been rejected by their parents and having received little in the way of loving personal attention. Furthermore, Hopf and colleagues were able to show that those who reported a high level of maternal attention tended to have internalized moral norms and rarely showed authoritarian aggression against weaker individuals. Those who had received little maternal attention made decisions in moral conflicts that were less norm oriented and more in their own interests and tended toward authoritarian aggression— characteristics identified in authoritarianism research as important preconditions for right-wing extremist attitudes.

Wahl and his colleagues found evidence that the emotional relationship to father and mother, combined with parental political attitudes and ethnic prejudices, influence the development of xenophobic attitudes, while each factor alone has no influence.[20] Where there is a positive parent-child relationship, parental orientations tend to be adopted, while a negative relationship tends to be associated with the development of contrary attitudes. But the relationship to the parents, parental attitudes in child raising, and family atmosphere have a clear and conspicuous effect on political orientations and attitudes, above all under especially difficult socialization conditions, for example, in cases of parental alcoholism and massive physical abuse.

Using a partial sample made up exclusively of violent adolescents, Wahl demonstrates that their xenophobia has emotional precursors in childhood.[21] In comparison with the neither violent nor xenophobic control group, the xenophobic violent offenders were more likely to have childhood memories of having felt uncomfortable dealing with strangers. Ethnic prejudices were then able to lock onto these initial fears of strangers, but generally did not manifest themselves as true xenophobia until adolescence. Right-wing extremist convictions, by contrast, did not correspond with specific behavioral disorders in childhood. But the findings of authoritarianism research that an authoritarian upbringing and the absence of the father can promote the development of authoritarian ideas were confirmed.[22]

It is certainly conspicuous that right-wing extremist violence is perpetrated above all by male adolescents.[23] Möller showed that both young men and young women strive to live up to traditional role expectations in order to form gender-typical identities in relationships of mutual recognition.[24] Hence, male adolescents tend to fulfill masculine functions that are anticipated and communicated to them in the parental home, school, media, and other socialization contexts and to underline this through a willingness and ability to fight. Female adolescents, in contrast, tend to "follow the clichés of femininity propounded by a society of male hegemony: considerateness, willingness to compromise, sexual attractiveness, etc."[25] According to Möller, violence is therefore a "male phenomenon" because male adolescents can use violence to establish their masculine identity, while female adolescents use other strategies to confirm their femininity.[26] By the same token, violence offers female adolescents a means to distance themselves from traditional role clichés.[27]

While socialization in the family has a great influence on the development of the preconditions for action, the influence of school and the media tends to be overestimated. Although right-wing extremist violent offenders have more than average problems at school, this is probably not a causal effect.[28] Rather, failures in school exacerbate family conflicts or favor a turn to groups espousing deviating norms and values, whereby one attraction of racist ideologies could be that devaluation of others is linked to increasing subjective self-esteem. In their time-series analyses of media reporting of xenophobic attacks, Lüdemann and Erzberger found clear evidence of a triggering effect, but media reports are probably not an actual cause of right-wing extremist violence.[29]

## Organization and political legitimation: Conditions for violent action

In groups espousing violence, adolescents can enjoy recognition and power that are often denied to them in the family and at school. The attraction of ideologies of unequal worth lies in being able to increase one's feeling of self-esteem by devaluing others for their inherited characteristics such as race or skin color.[30] The extent to which the violent potential in right-wing extremist groups can be activated depends at one level on individual socialization experiences and at another on the ideologies offered by elites, providing discursive footholds that lower the threshold to violence.[31] Public opinion can also legitimize right-wing extremist acts of violence if perpetrators feel they are "executing the will of the people." By means of regression analyses, Ohlemacher was able to demonstrate that public opinion on asylum policy had a strong effect on the development of violent xenophobic offenses in Germany.[32]

Indeed, the relationship between ideology and violence, which depends on the degree of politicization of the different groups, should not be forgotten here. In ideologically consolidated groups, violence has the function of enforcing ideology to create political power, and it is deployed deliberately and strategically. Such groups must be distinguished from groups (generally of adolescents) for whom more territorial power over social space is the prime concern. Here expressive violence tends to dominate, and fragments of ideology are drawn on for legitimation, sometimes with changing content. In the distribution of frequency of violence by the different violent groups, the bulk is opportunity-dependent violence perpetrated by cliques and skinhead groups that are not politically organized.[33]

## Interaction: Opportunity structures

Violence takes place in social situations characterized by power constellations in which perpetrator and victim (are forced to) act. A specific pattern of interaction is typical for such situations. What Levin and McDevitt describe for the American versions of hate crime violence also applies to right-wing extremist violence in Germany: it mostly involves excessive brutality, the victims have no personal connection with the perpetrators, the victims are arbitrary, and the situations are ones where the perpetrators outnumber the victims.[34] Furthermore, violent offenses with a right-wing extremist motivation almost always occur close to the perpetrators' home area.[35]

Using a daily time series with 857 measuring times, Lüdemann and Erzberger demonstrated that xenophobic offenses are registered overwhelmingly on weekends, when cliques and other groups meet in apartments, public squares, parks, bars, and discotheques.[36] These meetings are favored occasions for drinking bouts, often to the accompaniment of music with racist, xenophobic, and anti-Semitic lyrics.[37] In the group context, alcohol and music combine to create a mood of aggressive group solidarity that is simultaneously stimulating and disinhibiting and can motivate right-wing extremist acts of violence.

## Escalation: The dynamic of violence

At the microsocial level, escalation occurs within a restricted interaction context as an intensification of violence up to and including the killing of victims; in other words, violent action is unleashed, and those being attacked are individually "dehumanized." The mesosocial version expands the escalation to attack a whole group by stigmatizing them or breaking taboos.[38] This also depends on the extent to which the elites of a society help to legitimize an ideology of unequal worth by branding and judging immigrants (for example, by evaluating them as "useful" versus "useless"), thus potentially encouraging violent acts. In view of the complexities of the mechanisms that intensify and expand right-wing extremist violence, executive measures alone have few prospects of long-term success. Not least for this reason, the necessity of involving civil society in stemming right-wing extremist violence is being discussed.[39]

## Interpretation in the light of social disintegration theory

Right-wing extremist violence depends on various preconditions for action, contextual conditions, and escalation factors, which stand in complex relationships to one another. Bearing in mind the findings already described, we now move on to explain the function of right-wing extremist acts of violence for the perpetrators.

The starting point for our argument is the finding that intersubjective recognition is an existential human need.[40] In terms of the integration dimensions of social disintegration theory, we can distinguish three fundamental recognition needs that must be satisfied individually.[41] From this perspective, right-wing extremist violence can be understood as a "productive" way of dealing with individual recognition deficits. Although the consequences of denial of recognition needs are dealt with separately in the following, right-wing extremist violence can best be explained as a consequence of recognition deficits in all three central integration dimensions:

1. Participation in the material and cultural goods of society is experienced as positional recognition. Relevant objective factors here are sufficient access to work, housing, and consumer goods, and relevant subjective factors are adequate satisfaction with work and social position. Recognition deficits in this dimension can result from failure at school or work, low chances of social advancement, or the threat or fear of social decline. Such recognition deficits are found disproportionately often among violent right-wing extremist offenders. In this context, ideologies of unequal worth have a dual function. On the one hand, a positive self-image can be maintained by assigning to others the responsibility for one's own marginalized position. On the other, the feeling of self-esteem can be enhanced by devaluing other persons and groups. Finally, ideologies of unequal worth legitimize violence against the stigmatized persons and groups. One of the functions of acts of violence is to gain status in groups that approve of violence and in this way compensate for the lack of positional recognition.

2. Legal equality with others and the just regulation of conflicting interests are experienced as moral recognition. Here, negotiating and finding a balance of interests require that the affected social groups are both willing and able to participate. Recognition deficits in this dimension can result in particular from the assertion of priority rights by established residents, but also from racist, anti-Semitic, xenophobic, or heteropho-

bic convictions. Here, right-wing extremist violence has a dual function. On the one hand, it can be understood as a fight for "social justice," which from the perspective of a right-wing extremist can mean favoring the "white race" or returning to traditional gender roles. On the other, it can be understood as a fight for public and political attention in order to draw attention to the group's own marginalized situation.

3. Love and attention in close social relationships, the granting of freedoms, and the balancing of social support and normative demands are experienced as emotional recognition. Recognition deficits in this dimension can result in particular from direct and indirect experience of violence in the family and from active and passive denial of recognition by the parents. Such recognition deficits are found in almost all right-wing extremist violent offenders. In this context, adolescents' willingness to use violence can be explained first as an outcome of direct learning processes; second, as a consequence of development deficits such as a lack of empathy, ability to cooperate, or conflict-solving competence; and third, as an opportunity to compensate feelings of weakness by exercising power over the victims. Racism, anti-Semitism, ethnocentrism, xenophobia, heterophobia, and priority rights of established residents are also the result of learning processes. Ideologies of unequal worth find points of contact especially among adolescents who have formed authoritarian ideas or hostile attitudes and emotions as a consequence of emotional recognition deficits. Ideologies of unequal worth are functional, in particular, for identity forming among adolescents with such life experiences.

From the perspective of social disintegration theory, right-wing extremist acts of violence by adolescents are understood as the outcome of a process that is rooted in the family and that can escalate given specific conditions and opportunities. Although relatively few adolescents with positional, moral, or emotional deficits turn into right-wing extremist violent offenders, this can change depending on the conditions for action, opportunity structures, and escalation factors, especially given that hostile and right-wing extremist attitudes are widespread.

## Notes

1. Ideologies of unequal worth are at the heart of various facets of right-wing extremist ideologies such as racism (discrimination on the basis of biological differences), anti-Semitism (discrimination against people of Jewish origin or religion), ethnocentrism (a sense of superiority based on claims of cultural or economic achievement), xenophobia (exclusion of those of different ethnic origin from competition for work and housing, for example), heterophobia (fear of and discrimination against those who deviate from the norm), and giving established residents priority over "incomers." Heitmeyer, W. (1987). *Rechtsextremistische Orientierungen bei Jugendlichen. Empirische Ergebnisse zur politischen Sozialisation.* Weinheim/München: Juventa Verlag; Heitmeyer, W. (2003). Right-wing extremist violence. In W. Heitmeyer & J. Hagan (Eds.), *International handbook of violence research* (pp. 399–436). Dordrecht: Kluwer.

2. The GFE Survey is an ongoing annual survey of hostile attitudes in a representative sample of two thousand people in Germany, conducted over a period of ten years (2002–2011). The percentage figures quoted here are calculated under strict criteria, including only respondents who agreed "quite" or "fully" with all the statements in the corresponding scale. We thank Sandra Legge for the calculations.

3. Hüpping, S., & Asbrock, F. (2007). Deutsche Zustände–Unsere Gesellschaft: Unsicher und feindselig? Paper presented on a conference of the foundation of Friedrich Ebert in Saarbrücken (Germany); Endrikat, K. (2006). Jüngere Menschen, grössere Ängste, geringere Feindseligkeit. In W. Heitmeyer (Ed.), *Deutsche Zustände* (pp. 101–114). Frankfurt am Main: Suhrkamp.

4. Decker, O., Brähler, E., & Geissler, N. (2006). *Vom Rand zur Mitte. Rechtsextreme Einstellung und ihre Einflussfaktoren in Deutschland.* Berlin: Friedrich-Ebert-Stiftung.

5. The illustrated data are based on the Polizeiliche Kriminalstatistik Staatsschutz (PKS-S) and the Kriminalpolizeiliche Meldedienst Staatsschutz (KPMD-S) statistics and from 2001 on the Politisch motivierte Kriminalität (PMK) system of definitions. BMI. (2002). *Verfassungsschutzbericht 2001.* Berlin; Willems, H. (2002). Unabhängige Beobachtungsstelle für rechte Gewalt? Eine Verhinderungsgeschichte. In W. Heitmeyer (Ed.), *Deutsche Zustände.* (pp. 244–253). Frankfurt am Main: Suhrkamp.

6. BMI. (2007). *Verfassungsschutzbericht 2006.* Berlin, p. 21.

7. BMI. (2007). *Verfassungsschutzbericht 2006.* Berlin, p. 26.

8. Peucker, C., Gassebner, M., & Wahl, K. (2001). Analyse polizeilicher Ermittlungsakten zu fremdenfeindlichen, rechtsextremistischen und anti-semitischen Tatverdächtigen. In K. Wahl (Ed.), *Fremdenfeindlichkeit, Antisemitismus, Rechtsextremismus. Drei Studien zu Tatverdächtigen und Tätern.* Berlin: Bundesministerium des Inneren; Willems, H. (1994). Kollektive Gewalt gegen Fremde. Historische Episode oder Genese einer sozialen Bewe-

gung von rechts? In Bergmann, W. & Erb, R. (Eds.), *Neonazismus und rechte Subkultur* (pp. 209–226). Berlin: Metropol Verlag.

9. Peucker et al. (2001); Willems. (1994); Merton, R. (1968). Sozialstruktur und Anomie. In F. Sack & R. König (Eds.), *Kriminalsoziologie*. (pp. 282–313). Frankfurt am Main: Akademische Verlagsgesellschaft.

10. Heitmeyer, W. (2003). Right-wing extremist violence. In W. Heitmeyer & J. Hagan (Eds.), *International handbook of violence research* (pp. 399–436). Dordrecht: Kluwer.

11. Bjørgo, T. (1993). Terrorist violence against immigrants and refugees in Scandinavia: Patterns and motives. In T. Bjørgo (Ed.), *Racist violence in Europe* (pp. 29–45). New York: St. Martin's Press.

12. Hurrelmann, K.-J. (1995). *Einführung in die Sozialisationstheorie. Über den Zusammenhang von Sozialstruktur und Persönlichkeit.* Weinheim, Basel: Beltz Verlag; Hurrelmann, K.-J. (2002). *Einführung in die Sozialisationstheorie.* Weinheim, Basel: Beltz Verlag.

13. Heitmeyer, W., & Müller, J. (1995). *Fremdenfeindliche Gewalt junger Menschen. Biographische Hintergründe, soziale Situationskontexte und die Bedeutung strafrechtlicher Sanktionen.* Bonn: Forum-Verlag Godesberg.

14. Wendt, F., St. Lau, & H. L. Kröber. (2002). Rechtsradikale Gewalttäter. *Rechtsmedizin, 12,* 214–223.

15. Wendt et al. (2002).

16. Sutterlüty, F. (2002). *Gewaltkarrieren. Jugendliche im Kreislauf von Gewalt und Missachtung.* Frankfurt: Campus Verlag; Sutterlüty, F. (2004). Was ist eine "Gewaltkarriere"? *Zeitschrift für Soziologie, 33,* 266–284.

17. Hopf, C., & Hopf, W. (1997). *Familie, Persönlichkeit, Politik. Eine Einführung in die politische Sozialisation.* Weinheim, München: Juventa Verlag.

18. Hopf & Hopf. (1997).

19. Hopf & Hopf. (1997).

20. Wahl, K., Tramitz, C., & Blumtritt, J. (2001). *Fremdenfeindlichkeit. Auf den Spuren extremer Emotionen.* Opladen: Leske und Budrich.

21. Wahl, K. (2001). Entwicklungspfade von Aggression, Devianz, Fremdenfeindlichkeit und Rechtsextremismus. In K. Wahl (Ed.), *Fremdenfeindlichkeit, Antisemitismus, Rechtsextremismus. Drei Studien zu Tatverdächtigen und Tätern.* Berlin: BMI.

22. Wahl. (2001).

23. Willems, H., & Steigleder, S. (2003). *Täter-Opfer-Konstellationen und Interaktionen im Bereich fremdenfeindlicher, rechtsextremistischer und antisemitischer Gewaltdelikte. Eine Auswertung auf Basis quantitativer und inhaltsanalytischer Analysen polizeilicher Ermittlungsakten sowie von qualitativen Interviews mit Tätern und Opfern in NRW.* Trier. Research report. http://www1.polizeinrw.de/lka/stepone/data/downloads/42/00/00/studie_lang.pdf. Willems and Steigleder do find vague suggestions of right-wing extremist violence being increasingly exercised by young women.

24. Möller, K. (2001). *Coole Hauer und brave Engelein. Gewaltakzeptanz und Gewaltdistanzierung im Verlauf des frühen Jugendalters.* Opladen: Leske und Budrich.

25. Möller, K. (2002). Anerkennungsorientierung als pädagogische Antwort auf den Konnex von Männlichkeit und Gewalt. In B. Hafeneger, P. Henkenborg, & A. Scherr (Eds.), *Pädagogik der Anerkennung* (pp. 249–266). Schwalbach: Wochenschau Verlag, p. 255.

26. Möller. (2001, 2002). For the processes of entering, settling in, and leaving the right-wing extremist skinhead scene, see Möller, K., & Schuhmacher, N. (2007). *Rechte Glatzen. Rechtsextreme Orientierungs- und Szenezusammenhänge—Einstiegs-, Verbleibs- und Ausstiegsprozesse von Skinheads.* Wiesbaden: Verlag für Sozialwissenschaften.

27. Bruhns, K., & Wittmann, S. (2002). *Ich meine, mit Gewalt kannst du dir Despekt verschaffen. Mädchen und junge Frauen in gewaltbereiten Jugendgruppen.* Opladen: Leske und Budrich.

28. Fend, H. (1994). *Ausländerfeindlich-nationalistische Weltbilder und Aggressionsbereitschaft bei Jugendlichen in Deutschland und der Schweiz. Kontextuelle und personale Antecedensbedingungen. Zeitschrift für Sozialisationsforschung und Erziehungssoziologie, 14*(2), 131–162.

29. Lüdemann, C., & Erzberger, C. (1994). Fremdenfeindliche Gewalt in Deutschland. Zur zeitlichen Entwicklung und Erklärung von Eskalationsprozessen. *Zeitschrift für Rechtssoziologie, 15,* 169–190.

30. Heitmeyer, W. (1987). *Rechtsextremistische Orientierungen bei Jugendlichen. Empirische Ergebnisse und Erklärungsmuster einer Untersuchung zur politischen Sozialisation.* Weinheim, München: Juventa Verlag.

31. Esser, F., Scheufele, B., & Brosius, H.-B. (2002). *Fremdenfeindlichkeit als Medienthema und Medienwirkung. Deutschland im internationalen Scheinwerferlicht.* Wiesbaden: Westdeutscher Verlag; Willems. (1994).

32. Ohlemacher, T. (1994). Public opinion and violence against foreigners in the reunified Germany. *Zeitschrift für Soziologie, 23,* 222–236.

33. BMI (2006). *Verfassungsschutzbericht 2005.* Berlin.

34. Levin, J., & McDevitt, J. (1993). *Hate Crimes: The rising tide of bigotry and bloodshed.* New York: Plenum; Peucker et al. (2001).

35. Mentzel, T. (1998). *Rechtsextremistische Gewalttaten von Jugendlichen und Heranwachsenden in denen neuen Bundesländern. Eine empirische Untersuchung von Erscheinungsformen und Ursachen am Beispiel des Bundeslandes Sachsen-Anhalt.* München: Fink; Peucker et al. (2001); Willems, H., Eckert, R., Würtz, S., & Steinmetz, L. (1993). *Fremdenfeindliche Gewalt. Einstellungen, Täter, Konflikteskalation.* Opladen: Leske und Budrich.

36. Lüdemann et al. (1994); Willems et al. (1993).

37. Gassebner, M., Peucker, C., Schmidt, N., & Wahl, K, (2001). Analyse von Urteilsschriften zu fremdenfeindlichen, antisemitischen und rechtsextremistischen Straftätern. In K. Wahl (Ed.), *Fremdenfeindlichkeit, Antisemitismus, Rechtsextremismus. Drei Studien zu Tatverdächtigen und Tätern* (pp. 89–161). Berlin: BMI.

38. Brosius, H.-B., & Esser, F. (1995). *Eskalation durch Berichterstattung. Massenmedien und fremdenfeindliche Gewalt.* Opladen: Westdeutscher Verlag.

39. Eckert, R., & Willems, H. (2003). Escalation and de-escalation of social conflicts: The road to violence. In W. Heitmeyer & J. Hagan (Eds.), *International handbook of conflict and violence* (pp. 1181–1199). Dordrecht: Kluwer.

40. Honneth, A. (1995). *The struggle for recognition: The moral grammar of social conflicts.* Cambridge: Polity Press.
41. Anhut & Heitmeyer. (2006). *Disintegration, recognition and violence.* http://a.dorna.free.fr/RevueNo9/Rubrique2/R2SR1.htm

PETER SITZER *is a scientific assistant with the faculty of educational science at the University of Bielefeld.*

WILHELM HEITMEYER *is a professor of socialization at Bielefeld University, Germany, and head of the Institute for Interdisciplinary Research on Conflict and Violence.*

*Social disintegration theory provides convincing explanations for central findings of international research on violence. It can therefore be used as a basis for developing basic principles for social measures to reduce violence, including policy and professional social work concepts.*

# 11

# The role of social work in the context of social disintegration and violence

*Kurt Möller*

VIOLENCE IN its various facets is now seen worldwide as one of the main and most explosive social problems. At the same time, the connection between youth and violence is a key topic in international discourse and research on violence.

An abundance of academic studies has been published on the subject, especially over the past decade or two. Meanwhile, in most countries, a range, and in some cases a wide range, of social responses has emerged for dealing with youth violence through both intervention and prevention. Here, it is necessary to distinguish between basically repressive measures undertaken mainly by way of legislation and through police and judicial systems from efforts centered around effecting a long-term change in the social infrastructures, types of interpersonal communication, and individual dispositions that produce or encourage violence. Social work dealing with violence focuses mainly on the last type.

NEW DIRECTIONS FOR YOUTH DEVELOPMENT, NO. 119, FALL 2008 © WILEY PERIODICALS, INC.
Published online in Wiley InterScience (www.interscience.wiley.com) • DOI: 10.1002/yd.280

Even at the national level, there is good reason to doubt whether these measures can succeed in tackling the causes of violence because the links between research findings and practical activities are extremely tenuous and unsystematic.[1] This applies all the more so internationally, given the lack of reviews of the state of thematically relevant research with regard to the conclusions to be drawn for social work and aimed at highlighting the potential for international exchange and cooperation.

The aim of this article is to help fill that gap. In line with the topic of this volume, it focuses on the conclusions drawn from findings about the connection between social disintegration and violence in which juveniles are involved. It does so in two stages. It first provides an overview of basic international research findings on which a large degree of consensus is possible, placing each in an interpretive framework of disintegration theory. It then goes on to draw conclusions, extracting some basic principles for promising social work approaches.[2] It concludes by briefly recapitulating the main points of the article and outlining some prospects for collaboration between research and social work practice.

## Violence and disintegration: An overview of central international research findings

The limited scope of this article precludes a detailed description of the international social research findings on the connection between youth, disintegration, and violence. It therefore provides just a summarized selection of the most important facts, along with the possibilities for using disintegration theory to interpret them. Subject to this limitation, the following six points can be made about the acceptance of violence with regard to generational distribution, gender ratio, socioeconomic status, migration experience, education, and various disintegration experiences:[3]

1. Most violence in the world does not (and never did) emanate from children and juveniles; it stems from adults. Children and juveniles are disproportionately the victims of violence emanating from wars, so-called ethnic cleansing, famine, terrorism, neglect, maltreatment, child abuse, and other hardships that are produced and tolerated by adult society.[4] By focusing on the problem of youth violence, public and academic debate fails to give due consideration to how this problem behavior is weighted between the generations.

   As long as violence is seen mainly as an expression of severe adjustment problems specific to a particular age group, it is possible to conceal general structural problems with creating integrative living conditions by pointing to individual wrongdoing and subcultural deviations from the norm.[5] From the disintegration theory perspective, this point of view looks suspiciously like a diversionary maneuver to lay all the blame on the younger generation in order to preempt discussion of deep-seated social problems and the need for change. Thus, it largely avoids attributing adult society, especially its authorities and elites, with any responsibility for the ways in which the younger generation grows up or its integration.[6]

2. In both adults and adolescents, there is an immense preponderance of males among violent criminals and, to a slightly lesser degree, supporters of violence and people ready to use violence. With some differences depending on country, age group, milieu of origin, offense, and, in some cases, other modifying factors, boys and men carry out between roughly 75 and 99 percent of violent attacks. This male dominance is especially pronounced in aggravated assault and homicide.[7] Simultaneously, boys and men are disproportionately the victims of violence. The frequently ignored circumstance that violence is a problem of maleness rather than of youth may suggest that by focusing centrally on violence by juvenile perpetrators, adult discourse serves not least to reinforce hierarchical gender relationships in which males predominate. There is good empirical evidence to show

that male acceptance of violence is strongly encouraged by ideas of maleness that refer to traditional forms of hegemonic masculinity and enjoy wide social acceptance.[8]

This predominantly male affinity with violence has hardly been explained from the perspective of disintegration theory. However, it seems obvious to see this integration deficit as one of "overintegration." More precisely, it is particularist integration. Within the framework of hegemonic masculinity, youths and men still follow an archaic pattern of interpersonal dominance (represented, for instance, by the idea of a "fair man-to-man fight"). Although the majority still sees this as proof of masculinity, in modern society it has largely been relegated to symbolic modes of behavior (media consumption, weight training, martial arts, drinking contests, and so forth) and to experimental spaces that are specific to certain phases of life, such as playful childish tussles or adolescent boys' sparring. Apparently a male who engages in violence based on these masculinity norms can feel integrated as a "real man." Lacking equally attractive alternatives for a worthwhile masculinity, he enjoys the particularist integration provided by the violence-condoning reference group—usually a peer group but sometimes groups of male of different ages.

3. Socioeconomic status is significant inasmuch as one can ascertain that violence is most widespread among those who live in conditions that are socially and economically comparatively lowly and insecure.[9] Nonetheless, it has not been found to have a direct impact on acceptance of violence.[10] Family circumstances, the education and welfare system, and the labor market in particular, but probably also urban segregation,[11] leisure-time experience in peer groups, opportunity structures for the use of violence,[12] and individual dispositions can modify the impact of socioeconomic deprivation and the resulting frustration potential on the acceptance of violence.[13]

This finding underscores the need for an explanatory analytical model that, like disintegration theory, includes both individual and functional system integration aspects and social and collective social integration processes, and can be used to consider the dynamic interaction between and within these spheres of integration. This will make it possible to observe any supplementation, consolidation, and compensation effects produced by the interplay of integration dimensions and their elements and to identify their consequences for acceptance of violence. It will also reveal the highly significant roles played by both the structure of microsystemic relations and specific biographical experiences and by the institutional controllability of the level of violence in society.

4. At first sight, ethnic origin and cultural integration, along with migration status, whether personal or socially inherited from parents, appear to increase noticeably the probability of support for violence, propensity to violence, and violent activity.[14] Police statistics supply arguments in favor of reservations about "criminal foreigners,"[15] thereby contributing to a public debate in which xenophobic arguments can fall on ready ears.[16] Only a closer examination of the connection between migration experience and propensity to violence reveals that young migrants more frequently live in situations attended by violence, independent of ethnic and cultural affiliation. They are more likely than those who are native born to grow up in families where conflicts, violent conflict resolution, and authoritarian styles of upbringing prevail. They often occupy inferior positions in the education and vocational systems. They suffer disproportionately from unemployment and grim job prospects. On average, they have more problems in developing a stable identity than autochthonous youths, and they make greater use than the latter of media that glorify violence. They align themselves more closely with masculinity norms that legitimize and propagate violence, and they maintain stronger ties with their friends—in some circumstances, delinquent friends.[17] Baier, Pfeiffer, and Windzio have succeeded in showing empirically that among the especially violent problem group of individuals in Germany who have committed multiple

violent crimes, normative ideas of masculinity and honor that legitimize violence play a decisive role. These ideas develop in the context of consumption of violence-oriented media and delinquent peer group relations, and they become fixed. Again, the attractiveness of such media, norms, and ties with friends is attributable above all to the experience of parental violence.[18]

Interpreted from the disintegration theory perspective, the fact that young migrants and indigenous people are disproportionately involved in violence is clearly attributable to the integration deficits they have suffered in central social spheres. Particularist-type ethnic and cultural integration, which is explosive, among other things, in terms of favoring violence, must thus be interpreted not least as taking advantage of socialization traditions and opportunity structures whose allure is not least a consequence of actual or perceived exclusion from the majority society. Thus, when looking at the reasons for reference to ethnic and cultural patterns that favor violence, as in the case of reference to patterns of masculinity that favor violence, one sees a lack of alternatives for creative and recognition experiences within the framework of normative and cultural patterns of a universal cut.

5. Education is a highly significant factor in determining whether someone develops an acceptance of violence. However, only on superficial consideration is educational level in the sense of the formal qualification achieved or aspired to a deciding factor. One must indeed assume that it is no coincidence that the very people who live in the socialization constellations already noted are concentrated in the especially violence-prone lower types of school and vocational courses, because those constellations have a major impact on the course of people's lives.[19] Moreover, Heyder showed empirically that it is not so much just additional education as empathy and cognitive complexity that protect individuals from hostile attitudes such as racism, xenophobia, or anti-Semitism that can be pinpointed as preceding the acceptance of violence.[20] An individual who succeeds in

acquiring or developing such capabilities even in adverse educational circumstances appears to be as far removed from such hostile orientations as individuals with higher education. Other social competences have a similar effect: above all, establishing a realistic sense of self-esteem, openness to and curiosity about things that are new, tolerance of frustration, ambivalence and ambiguity, role distance, functioning emotional management, including especially control of emotions and impulses, willingness to take responsibility, and verbal conflict skills.[21]

In the context of disintegration theory, however, it is not so much this finding as such that is significant as the question of how deficits, or advances, in competence emerge. Here, one must assume that the integration circumstances, in particular the socioemotional frame of reference in which the particular subject is socialized, play a key role. A person who has had meaningful experience of recognized self-efficacy and personal esteem in the context of prosocial relationship networks, thereby gaining a secure identity, does not feel compelled to go about stabilizing his or her identity by means of hostile and violent orientations.

6. In connection with the factors already noted and in part pointing beyond them, mention must be made of further disintegration experiences that have the effect of encouraging violence. Among the most important are feelings of powerlessness and lack of influence in the political sphere, blocked access to labor and consumer markets, and the failure of social institutions responsible for establishing and maintaining security, justice, fairness, solidarity, education, and the satisfaction of cultural needs.[22]

Disintegration theory assumes that the fact of being subjectively affected by these factors, along with the aspects of integration problems noted, feed into balances of recognition. These are seen as the ultimate, decisive foundation on which the subject develops his or her orientation and determines how to act. It seems plausible that balances drawn up on the basis of the subject's experience act as orientation and action control systems. Especially in an individualized society with its rapidly increasing scope and need for the subject to make decisions, and where biographical fit is the ultimate standard by which new experiences and impressions gained during the course of life are evaluated, the significance of accruing self-reflections increases. Nonetheless, one questions whether the concept of balances of recognition adequately describes the challenges facing the individual in the course of life in respect of orientation and the need to make decisions.

Heitmeyer himself assumes an action and socialization theory model of the "subject productively assimilating reality."[23] Yet this model "places the human subject in a social and ecological context that is subjectively absorbed and assimilated and thereby impacts on the individual yet at the same time is always influenced, changed and *shaped* by the individual."[24] If the social capacity to act is seen as the objective of the socialization process, neither social integration nor social recognition can fully meet it. Rather, at the interface between autonomy and heteronomy and individuation and integration, a process of building independent identity takes place. On the one hand, this process is aimed at ensuring unmistakable, self-determined action and thus personal identity, and on the other at enabling the subject to connect to social demands and intersubjective contexts and thus social identity.[25] At least two further important codetermining factors exist. First, to examine such processes from an angle that focuses solely on the shaping of the relationship between freedom and bonding in fields of integration is to lose sight of the subject's instrumental conflicts with the natural and material world and their potential for building independent identity and, consequently, self-worth. Yet people are not just social beings but—certainly according to the concept of interaction theory—"implemental animals" that acquire awareness of self primarily by dealing with objects and embedding them cooperatively.[26] The "conditions of life" with which the subject interacts during the socialization process are without a doubt of a material as well as a social nature. Second, since the development of personality is by definition a process, the acquisition and expansion of individual skills is of central, self-worth-generating significance. Along with instrumental competences, personal and social competences must be developed in order to facilitate autonomous, emotionally harmonious, yet socially compatible, even respectable, self-orientation and action.

This can be taken account of by an understanding of socialization that comprehends biographical life activity as a process of autonomous yet socially buffered scope to organize one's own life. In everyday language, from the subject's viewpoint, having the scope to organize one's life means aiming to take control of one's life by means of positive action and not to become dependent, or the plaything of outside forces. At the same time, efforts to control one's life should not leave one socially isolated. Accordingly, having scope to organize one's life also means striving to maintain social contact and to acquire and develop capabilities that permit one to secure and optimize control and integration.

Thus, it is comprehensive balances of scope to organize rather than balances of recognition that are responsible for setting biographical directions, including possibly toward acceptance of violence. Such balances of scope to organize one's life have factual, social, and temporal dimensions in that they follow the subject's aspirations to control the objective and natural world, develop for themselves an accepted position in the social setup, and by doing so acquire and improve a personal capacity to act and experience. However, aspirations can differ widely in scope. The aim is not in every case to develop and augment options for action but to achieve a basic feeling of being able to control one's life, a feeling from which a certainty of interpretation, orientation, behavior, and action can be drawn that is open to argument and flexible in responding to situations. Moreover, every subject is geared toward psychophysical experiencing of positive valence.[27] In detail, the point is to develop individual modes of action so as to enable:

- Control over one's own life to be experienced and secured
- Integration in understanding-oriented communication and cooperation contexts to be experienced

- Competences to structure experiences, including the securing of integration, reflexivity, empathy, toleration of ambivalence, communicativeness, control of emotions, and so forth to be acquired, applied, safeguarded, and expanded

Only in such an action theory–inspired model of such balances of scope to organize one's life are the findings of Brezina fully interpretable.[28] These show that a me-first attitude that is clearly conducive to violence grows out of a lack of recognition. To equate, citing Agnew, such an "attitude" with "autonomy" and to understand "autonomy" as merely a desire "to be free from the control of others" is to overlook the bogus nature of apparent "autonomy" of this kind.[29] It obstructs the path toward grasping this pseudoautonomy as an expression and consequence of an experienced lack of realizable, autonomous empowerment in the sense of a capacity for productive, creative processing of reality. In this respect, one should examine whether experiences of an almost complete or relative lack of possibilities to organize one's life autonomously regarding control over one's life, integration, and the development of competence might not explain the acceptance of violence more fully than do denials of recognition.

## Consequences for how society deals with violence and the role of social work

The findings just outlined lead to conclusions that cast some doubt on prevailing ideas and practice about measures to reduce violence. This applies to both the way in which society deals with the problem of violence and social work in particular. For reasons of space, I summarize the most important consequences in seven points:[30]

1. A sustained reduction in violence presupposes human rights foundations. This applies to all fields of policy, but especially

to interior, security, legal, and social policy. In any case, human rights foundations are inadequate or nonexistent wherever:

- Social inequalities are structurally anchored, but especially where violation of the human rights of certain population groups enjoys far-reaching social acceptance (in some African countries, for instance)
- The responsibility of organs of state for establishing and maintaining public order and security is disputed among the population
- These organs are instruments of an undemocratic ruling apparatus, serve different political interest groups, or act clearly in the interest, if not actually in the service, of economic elites[31]
- They act the role of democratic authorities but because of their own weakness are unable to assert themselves against armed groups
- They are largely corrupt and cooperate with organized crime[32]
- A national welfare system fails to function, or does so inadequately, so that fundamental rights to freedom, equal treatment, and social justice cannot be guaranteed equally for all members of society

As agreed internationally by its main sponsors, actors, and educational institutes, social work explicitly sees itself as a human rights profession that advocates assertion of these rights and integration, and therefore nonviolent conditions.[33] Accordingly, it sees itself as a supporter of people's interests in and capacity to shape their lives as they so determine. Nonetheless, in this role, it rapidly runs up against limits unless it can build on legal and security policy structures that fundamentally safeguard human rights and protect every member of society's right to personal integrity, most urgently to physical integrity. Politicians must not be released from their responsibility for this.

NEW DIRECTIONS FOR YOUTH DEVELOPMENT • DOI: 10.1002/yd

2. Measures to prevent or intervene in violence are no substitute for good social policy. We now know that repressive measures run up against their limits at the latest when it is necessary to remove the causes of violence.[34] We also know the high cost of such measures.[35] Yet social work as an element of the welfare system in various Western countries cannot in the long run continue mending the failures of social policy and social wrongs. Rather, social work needs a reliable social policy foundation in order to exert a sustained positive influence on power relations. This primacy of social policy applies regardless of the national status and stage of development of social work, which differs, sometimes greatly, from country to country, even in industrialized countries. The cuts in welfare services being implemented in a large number of Western countries, in accordance with neoliberal political views, are therefore proving totally counterproductive.[36] The probability of violence occurring increases in line with the extent to which such cuts are implemented, as is currently evident, for instance, in some regions of eastern Germany. First, they lead to the collapse of the very bridges to integration that it is a central task of violence-reduction measures to build, and not just from a disintegration theory viewpoint. Second, they thwart the development of alternative modes of integration, which, given the erosion of traditional paths to integration (such as integration into "normal working conditions," "normal biographies," and "normal families"), is urgently needed because the practice of segregation suppresses the prospect of integration.

Admittedly, reorganization of the state welfare system in Western countries such as Germany also gives rise to opportunities for closer cooperation between institutions, and in particular for rebalancing the relationship between civil society and social work. As far as dealing with violence is concerned, opportunities exist for both civil society actors in local adult society and youths themselves to play a greater role within the framework of comprehensive preventive approaches on a multi-issue basis.[37]

3. It is not enough to tackle violence indiscriminately. Even without a critical appraisal of relevant approaches and evaluations of them (still undertaken far too seldom in Europe, at least), approaches will necessarily fall short of their goal unless they systematically appraise deficits in scope for people to organize their own lives and thus also in integration and recognition, or if they overlook the dynamic interaction of integration dimensions. This happens if they are selective and short term and are not integrated into a broad, long-term, overall concept for dealing with violence in society that pays equal attention to the macrolevel of structures, the mesolevel of institutions, and the microlevel of "small life worlds" and biography. Since this type of conceptually saturated national broadband concept cannot be seen to exist in any country in the world at present, despite nationwide programs in some countries such as Germany,[38] it is time for a fundamental review and realignment. This will include making the bodies, programs, and projects involved in violence reduction—for example in kindergartens, schools, and youth work—network and consult more closely. Adults too must be involved as a target group to a greater extent than previously, as must the field of family and parental education work. Moreover, a composite concept must include an international perspective, if only because the problems of violence have become internationalized (for example, cross-border crimes of violence, transnational cooperation between extremists).

4. The idea of demonstrating the supposed senselessness of violence is based on false premises. On the other hand, taking into account the previous analyses in this volume, it seems promising to take as a starting point an understanding of violence that sees acceptance of violence as an element and outcome of a problematic process of productive assimilation of reality that serves subjectively to satisfy the need for scope to organize one's own life. These balances of scope to organize one's life must be examined more systematically than hitherto, not least in their milieu-, migration-, and gender-specific forms, and

must be treated accordingly in social work. That acceptance of violence serves to give sense to these balances is highly significant for social work strategies to combat violence. It shows that neither moral appeals nor well-meaning attempts to explain the sense and benefit of nonviolence or behavior therapy responses lead to the desired results. Rather, concepts of violence reduction must be developed in pursuit of the question of how the sense produced through acceptance of violence can be replaced by the offer of individually and socially reconcilable connotations. Among other things, this entails pursuing far more intensively than hitherto concepts that take a gender-reflective approach, especially regarding males, and that take ethnic and cultural orientations into account.

5. Selective strategies come to nothing. Rather, for social work with the aim of reducing violence that starts from the above premises, at least three central fields of action open up. First, in the field of life control, the main concern is to support addressees in acquiring and maintaining orientation capacity, in being able to feel self-efficacy and to act with confidence, in being able to influence and plan their conditions of life, and in developing and stabilizing their identity to the extent where the consistency, coherence, and continuity of experience of self is not called into question.

Second, in the field of integration, it is of prime importance to ensure that personal integrity is maintained to facilitate experiences of belonging, participation as defined by disintegration theory, and, as far as possible, social support, to communicate self-worth, while simultaneously making it possible to experience the validity of fundamental moral rules such as justice and nonviolence.

Since everyday experiences generally have more orientation-forming impact than short-term educational programs, the development of personal and social competences, the third field, must be seen as an important component of activities aimed at securing control and integration, such as conflict regulation.

6. To be "anti" alone is not enough. If scientific knowledge shows clearly that control, integration, and competence deficits are the essential causal links in the acceptance of violence, that knowledge has implications for antiviolence approaches in social work, in terms of developing functional equivalents in precisely those areas for and with the people affected. Thus, a concept of admonishing perpetrators of violence has no greater prospect of success than naked repression. There is no way around providing the younger generation with conditions of life and socialization in which violence gradually becomes (at least relatively) superfluous because sufficient alternative forms of experiencing control, integration, and competence are available.

7. Reactionism is not a perspective, since one can conclude from the above points that social work to combat violence will be a lost cause as long as the profession exhausts itself in attempts to provide individual therapy to those who are susceptible to violence. Inasmuch as the causes of violence are structurally anchored, the social work profession's cause-related strategy for dealing with violence-related social problems cannot avoid seeing its work as infrastructural work designed for the long term. Along with work on individual cases, group work, and activities in the local community, a professional strategy of political involvement is essential. Ultimately, only this will enable responsibility for ensuring that young people grow up in nonviolent conditions to be honored by bringing the profession's specific competences, such as social space perspective, reference to addressees, life-world orientation, and empowerment strategies, into concepts that integrate various institutions, fields of work, and professional responsibilities.

## Conclusion

Violence is a product of structural, interactional, and individual processes. The theory of social disintegration provides a concept with the help of which the interaction of these process levels can

be observed. In addition to its great power to explain violent phenomena, it provides a stimulating scientific backdrop for developing practical strategies for dealing with the social problem of
violence. Social work, not least, can profit from this, since it needs
an integrative approach that makes the interplay of socioeconomic,
political, cultural and socialization, individual, and situational factors the basis of its work.[39]

Although there is a need for further development,[40] with the
help of the disintegration approach, the social work profession
can realign itself and become more cause related. In doing so, it can
recall its basic function as working on social inequality and injustice or establishing social equality and justice. To the extent that
the concept is pursued internationally and shown to be sustainable,
it can enable the profession to see beyond individual national hori-
zons, find transnational points of contact, and thereby equip itself
to respond to the increasing internationalization of problems of
violence. Above all, by recourse to this approach, social work will
have opportunities, at least conceptually, to reduce the extent to
which it is used as a firefighter for problems that have been caused
elsewhere—in this case, violence.

## Notes

1. Compare, for example, for Germany: Möller, K. (2002). *Pädagogische und
sozialarbeiterische Ansätze der Stärkung von Integrationspotenzialen zur Bearbeitung
von Rechtsextremismus, Fremdenfeindlichkeit und Gewalt: Erziehungs- und sozialar-
beitswissenschaftliche Expertise für das BMWF zum Forschungsverbund "Stärkung
von Integrationspotenzialen einer modernen Gesellschaft."* Unpublished manuscript,
Esslingen and Bielefeld.

2. Reasons of space preclude providing in addition a critical description of
the landscape of existing youth violence prevention and intervention
approaches from an international perspective. For an overview, see Prothrow-
Stith, D. (2002). Youth violence prevention in America: Lessons from 15 years
of public health prevention work. In M. Tienda & W. J. Wilson (Eds.), *Youth
in cities: A cross-national perspective* (pp. 165–190). Cambridge: Cambridge University Press; White, R. (2002). Youth crime, community development, and
social justice. In M. Tienda & W. J. Wilson (Eds.), *Youth in cities: A cross-
national perspective* (pp. 138–164). Cambridge: Cambridge University Press;
Council of Europe (Ed.). (2007). *Young people from lower-income neighbourhoods:
Guide to new policy approaches.* Strasbourg: Council of Europe Publishing.

3. Here *acceptance of violence* is used as an umbrella term for support for violence, propensity to violence, and violent activity, where violence is understood as illegitimate physical or psychological harm to the integrity of another person.

4. See, for example, Heitmeyer and Anhut, and Huguet and Szabó de Carvalho in this volume.

5. See also Males, M. (1996). *The scapegoat generation: America's war on adolescents.* Monroe, ME: Common Courage Press.

6. See also Cockburn in this volume.

7. See many of the contributions in this volume. Also see, for example, Junger-Tas, J. (1994). Delinquency in thirteen Western countries: Some preliminary conclusions. In J. Junger-Tas, G.-J. Terlouw, & M. Klein (Eds.), *Delinquent behavior among young people in the Western world: First results of the international self-report delinquency study* (pp. 371–379). Amsterdam: Kugler Publications.

8. Connell, R. W. (1995). *Masculinities.* Cambridge: Polity Press.

9. See, for example, World Health Organization. (2002). *World report on violence and health.* Geneva: World Health Organization; White. (2002).

10. See also Legge in this volume.

11. See Oberti in this volume.

12. See, for example, Sitzer and Heitmeyer in this volume.

13. On the interaction of these risk factors, see also Farrington, D. (1996). The explanation and prevention of youthful offending. In J. Hawkins (Ed.), *Delinquency and crime: Current theories* (pp. 68–148). Cambridge: Cambridge University Press.

14. See in this volume: Zdun; Baier and Pfeiffer; and Mesch, Turjeman, and Fishman. See also Hazelhurst, K. (Ed.). (1995). *Perceptions of justice.* Aldershot: Avebury; Tonry, M. (1997). Ethnicity, crime, and immigration. In M. Tonry (Ed.), *Ethnicity, crime, and immigration: Comparative and cross-national perspectives* (pp. 1–30). Chicago: University of Chicago Press.

15. See for the German example most recently: Bundeskriminalamt. (Ed.). (2007). *Polizeiliche Kriminalstatistik 2006.* Wiesbaden: Bundeskriminalamt; Bundesministerium des Innern and Bundesministerium der Justiz (2006). *Zweiter Periodischer Sicherheitsbericht.* Berlin.

16. For a critical treatment, see Mansel, J. (2007). Kriminelle Ausländer? Fremdenfeindlichkeit, Anzeigeverhalten und Kontrollpolitik in den Bundesländern. In W. Heitmeyer (Ed.), *Deutsche Zustände* (pp. 169–191). Frankfurt am Main: Suhrkamp.

17. See above all in this volume, Baier and Pfeiffer, but also Zdun; and Mesch, Turjeman, and Fishman.

18. Baier, D., Pfeiffer, C., & Windzio, M. (2006). Jugendliche mit Migrationshintergrund als Opfer und Täter. In W. Heitmeyer & M. Schröttle (Eds.), *Gewalt: Beschreibungen, Analyse, Prävention* (pp. 240–268). Bonn: Bundeszentrale für politische Bildung. See also Baier and Pfeiffer in this volume.

19. Mills, M., & Blossfeld, H.-P. (2005). Globalization, uncertainty, and the early life course: A theoretical framework. In H.-P. Blossfeld, E. Klijzing, M. Mills, & K. Kurz (Eds.), *Globalization, uncertainty and youth in society.* London: Routledge.

20. Heyder, A. (2003). Bessere Bildung, bessere Menschen? Genaueres Hinsehen hilft weiter. In W. Heitmeyer (Ed.), *Deutsche Zustände* (pp. 78–99). Frankfurt am Main: Suhrkamp.

21. See, for example, Hay, D. F., Castle, J., & Jewett, J. (1996). Character development. In M. Rutter & D. F. Hay (Eds.), *Development through life: A handbook for clinicans* (pp. 319–349). Oxford: Blackwell Science; Eisenberg, N., Losoya, S., & Spinrad, T. (2003). Affect and prosocial responding. In R. J. Davidson, K. R. Scherer, & H. H. Goldsmith (Eds.), *Handbook of affective sciences* (pp. 787–803). New York: Oxford University Press; Möller, K. (2001). *Coole Hauer und brave Engelein: Gewaltakzeptanz und Gewaltdistanzierung im Verlauf des frühen Jugendalters.* Opladen: Leske + Budrich; Möller, K., & Schuhmacher, N. (2007). *Rechte Glatzen: Rechtsextreme Szene- und Orientierungszusammenhänge– Einstiegs-, Verbleib- und Ausstiegsprozesse von Skinheads.* Wiesbaden: VS-Verlag; Wahl, K. (2007). *Vertragen oder schlagen? Biografien jugendlicher Gewalttäter als Schlüssel für eine Erziehung zur Toleranz in Familie, Kindergarten und Schule.* Berlin: Cornelsen Scriptor.

22. See the numerous references in this volume and empirical evidence in Heitmeyer, W. (2002, 2003, 2005, 2006, 2007, 2008). *Deutsche Zustände.* Frankfurt am Main: Suhrkamp.

23. See, for example, Sitzer and Heitmeyer in this volume.

24. Hurrelmann, K. (1986). *Einführung in die Sozialisationstheorie.* Weinheim and Basle: Beltz, 64; Hurrelmann, K. (1988). *Social structure and personality development.* Cambridge: Cambridge University Press, italics added.

25. Goffman, E. (1963). *Stigma: Notes on the management of spoiled identity.* Upper Saddle River, NJ: Prentice Hall.

26. Mead, G. H. (1938). *The philosophy of the act.* (C. W. Morris and others, Eds.). Chicago: University of Chicago.

27. It cannot be assumed that balancing processes are necessarily rationally controlled and conscious. As well as the normative understanding of the "wholeness" of people that is widespread in social work, recent findings in neurology and the psychology of decision making also give reason to believe that the self-reflection that is active in balancing processes uses at least three functional areas: (1) the cognitive self-contemplation of consciousness, (2) sensations in the sense of witnessing corporeal processes, and (3) reflexes in the sense of nonconscious responses to sensory stimuli. Damasio, A. (2005). *Descartes' error* (10th anniversary ed.). New York: Penguin Books; Damasio, A. (2003). *Looking for Spinoza: Joy, sorrow and the feeling brain.* Orlando, FL: Harcourt; Damasio, A. (1999). *The feeling of what happens: Body and emotion in the making of consciousness.* Orlando, FL: Harcourt; Gigerenzer, G. (2007). *Gut feelings.* New York: Penguin. To overstate the case a little, the self-reference that shapes a person's own life is organized not only by consideration of the question, "Where do I stand, and where do I want to go?" but also by answers to the question, actually unasked, "What does me good?" or, more precisely, "What feels good?" So the character of violence must be considered as sensory experience, as "embodied social practice," and thus as a positively experienced momentary condition of the body. Lyng, S. (2004). Crime, edgework and corporeal transaction. *Theoretical Criminology, 8,* 359–375.

28. See his contribution in this volume.

29. Agnew, R. (1984). *Autonomy and delinquency. Sociological Perspectives, 27,* 219–240 (225).

30. For further detail and more on practice, see also Möller, K. (2007). Soziale Arbeit gegen Menschenfeindlichkeit: Lebensgestaltung über funktionale Äquivalenzen und Kompetenzentwicklung. In W. Heitmeyer (Ed.), *Deutsche Zustände:* (pp. 294–311). Frankfurt am Main: Suhrkamp.

31. See Zdun in this volume on conditions in Russia and Brazil.

32. See Huguet in this volume on the role of the police in Rio de Janeiro.

33. International Federation of Social Workers (IFSW) and International Association of Schools of Social Work (IASSW). (2001). *International definition of social work.* http://www.iassw-aiets.org.

34. Council of Europe. (2007); White. (2002). For an illustrative example, see Huguet in this volume.

35. Prothrow-Stith. (2002).

36. Thome, H., & Birkel, C. (2007). *Sozialer Wandel und Gewaltkriminalität.* Wiesbaden: Verlag für Sozialwissenschaften.

37. Council of Europe. (2007).

38. www.vielfalt-tut-gut.de and www.kompetent-fuer-demokratie.de.

39. One example in this context is the project that won the 2008 Deutscher Kinder- und Jugendhilfepreis (German Youth Work Award). For more detail, see Bleiss, K., Möller, K., Peltz, C., Rosenbaum, D., & Sonnenberg, I. (2004). Distanz(ierung) durch Integration– Neue konzeptionelle Grundlagen für aufsuchende Arbeit mit rechtsextrem bzw. menschenfeindlich orientierten Jugendlichen. *Neue Praxis, 6,* 568–590; Gulbins, G., Möller, K., Rosenbaum, D., & Stewen, I. (2007). "Denn sie wissen nicht, was sie tun?" Evaluation aufsuchender Arbeit mit rechtsextrem und menschenfeindlich orientierten Jugendlichen. *Deutsche Jugend, 12,* 526–534.

40. On other aspects, see note 27.

KURT MÖLLER *is professor of social work at the Esslingen University of Applied Sciences.*

# Index

German school survey (2005): background information on, 152–156; disintegration and violence questions used in, 158t–161; on ethnic homogeneity, 162; model explaining prevalence of violence, 164fig; results of, 163–166; sample description used in, 156–158

German youth: criminal gang membership of, 47, 48–49; right-wing extremist violence among, 169–182; school survey (2005) on violence and immigrant, 156–166; street culture of, 43

Germany: criminal gang membership in, 47, 48–49; ethnicity/racial factor in violence in, 44–45; migration, disintegration and socialization of immigrant youth in, 152–156; reorganization of state welfare system in, 198; right-wing extremist violence among adolescents in, 169–182; school survey (2005) on immigrant youth violence, 156–166; street culture in, 43; war refugees immigrating to, 151–152

Gostomski, B. von, 152

GPAE (Grupamento de Policiamento em Áreas Especiais) [Brazil], 102–105, 107

Group Focused Emmity (GFE) survey [2006], 169

Hagan, J., 174
Hall, S., 81
Hanover survey (2006), 161
Hao, L., 131
Heitmeyer, W., 1, 5, 6, 8, 14, 25, 34, 37, 39, 82, 98, 99, 123, 129, 134, 169, 174, 185, 194
Heyder, A., 192
High Authority for the Fight Against Discrimination and for Equality (la HALDE) [France], 66
Homicide rates: gender and age differences in, 17; global and regional differences in, 18
Hopf, C., 175, 176
Huguet, C., 3, 11, 93, 109
Husband, C., 79

Immigrant youth: bilingualism of, 131–132; disintegration and violence in Germany among, 151–166; family functioning and impact on, 134–135; perceived discrimination of, 133–134, 146; social identity formation of, 131–132; study on Israeli, 135–147. See also Ethnicity/racial factors; Youth

Immigrants: acculturation conflicts faced by, 130, 132–133; bilingualism of, 131–132; family functioning among, 134–135; French 2005 riots and 2006 student movement and role of, 55, 59–66; French regroupement familial (reunification of family), 58; perceived discrimination of, 133–134, 146; post-World War II French, 58–59; social identity formation of, 131–132

Inequality. See Social inequalities
Institutional dimension of social integration, 26–27t, 29–30
Integration. See Social integration
Inter-University Consortium of Political and Social Research, 118
International Labour Office, 20
Israel: acculturation process into, 130, 132–133; immigration from FSU (former Soviet Union) to, 135; melting pot model of, 135, 145
Israeli immigrant youth study: background information on, 135–136; data and methods used in, 136–138; discussion of, 145–147; results of, 139t–145

Jahangir, A., 101
Johnston, J., 118
Juvenile homicide rates: gender and age differences in, 17; global and regional differences in, 18

Laïcite (secularism) movement (France), 56
Lambert, W. E., 131
Language use: immigrant, 131–132; Israeli immigrant youth study on, 138, 142t, 144t
Learning theory, 31–32
Legge, S., 6, 7, 17, 24

# Notes for Contributors

After reading this issue, you might be interested to become a contributor. *New Directions for Youth Development: Theory, Practice, and Research* is a peer-reviewed quarterly publication focusing on contemporary issues inspiring and challenging the field of youth development. A defining focus of the journal is the relationship among theory, research, and practice. In particular, *NDYD* is dedicated to recognizing resilience as well as risk, and healthy development of our youth as well as the difficulties of adolescence. The journal is also interested in applications of youth development to education and schools, and is a leading voice in afterschool and out-of-school time scholarship. The journal is intended as a forum for provocative discussion that reaches across the worlds of academia, service, philanthropy, and policy.

In the tradition of the New Directions series, each volume of the journal addresses a single, timely topic, although special issues covering a variety of topics are occasionally commissioned. We welcome submissions of both volume topics and individual articles. All articles should address the implications of theory for practice and research directions, and how these arenas can better inform one another. Articles may focus on any aspect of youth development; all theoretical and methodological orientations are welcome.

If you would like to be an *issue editor*, please submit an outline of no more than four pages that includes a brief description of your proposed topic and its significance along with a brief synopsis of individual articles (including tentative authors and a working title for each chapter).

If you would like to be an *author*, please submit first an abstract of no more than 1,500 words. Send this to the editorial manager.

For all prospective issue editors or authors:

- Please make sure to keep accessibility in mind, by illustrating theoretical ideas with specific examples and explaining technical terms in nontechnical language. A busy practitioner who may not have an extensive research background should be well served by our work.
- Please keep in mind that references should be limited to twenty-five to thirty. Authors should make use of case examples to illustrate their ideas, rather than citing exhaustive research references. You may want to recommend two or three key articles, books, or Web sites that are influential in the field, to be featured on a resource page. This can be used by readers who want to delve more deeply into a particular topic.
- All reference information should be listed as endnotes, rather than including author names in the body of the article or footnotes at the bottom of the page. The endnotes are in APA style.

Please visit http://www.pearweb.org for more information.

Gil G. Noam
*Editor-in-Chief*

**NEW DIRECTIONS FOR YOUTH DEVELOPMENT
IS NOW AVAILABLE ONLINE AT WILEY INTERSCIENCE**

## What is Wiley InterScience?

*Wiley InterScience* is the dynamic online content service from John Wiley & Sons delivering the full text of over 300 leading scientific, technical, medical, and professional journals, plus major reference works, the acclaimed *Current Protocols* laboratory manuals, and even the full text of select Wiley print books online.

## What are some special features of Wiley InterScience?

*Wiley InterScience Alerts* is a service that delivers table of contents via e-mail for any journal available on Wiley InterScience as soon as a new issue is published online.
*Early View* is Wiley's exclusive service presenting individual articles online as soon as they are ready, even before the release of the compiled print issue. These articles are complete, peer-reviewed, and citable.
*CrossRef* is the innovative multi-publisher reference linking system enabling readers to move seamlessly from a reference in a journal article to the cited publication, typically located on a different server and published by a different publisher.

## How can I access Wiley InterScience?

Visit http://www.interscience.wiley.com

*Guest Users* can browse Wiley InterScience for unrestricted access to journal Tables of Contents and Article Abstracts, or use the powerful search engine.
*Registered Users* are provided with a *Personal Home Page* to store and manage customized alerts, searches, and links to favorite journals and articles. Additionally, Registered Users can view free Online Sample Issues and preview selected material from major reference works.
*Licensed Customers* are entitled to access full-text journal articles in PDF, with select journals also offering full-text HTML.

## How do I become an Authorized User?

*Authorized Users* are individuals authorized by a paying Customer to have access to the journals in Wiley InterScience. For example, a university that subscribes to Wiley journals is considered to be the Customer. Faculty, staff, and students authorized by the university to have access to those journals in Wiley InterScience are Authorized Users. Users should contact their Library for information on which Wiley journals they have access to in Wiley InterScience.

**ASK YOUR INSTITUTION ABOUT WILEY INTERSCIENCE TODAY!**